Opening up
Nahum

CLIVE ANDERSON

DayOne

Opening up
Nahum

CLIVE ANDERSON

'Clive Anderson has done a fine job in research to illuminate the historical background of the prophet Nahum, small in volume, but important in principles, for the majority of church members to whom the book may be rather obscure. He then takes these principles of Nahum and applies them to New Testament teaching and to modern life. It's a good, interesting read, but more importantly, the study questions should cause the thinking reader to apply the principles of Nahum to personal and church life. I think it is especially good for a local church Bible study group.'

Rev. Herbert E. Apel, M.A.,
New Testament Literature, Wheaton College, Illinois, USA; retired missionary in four European countries, former Representative in Europe for The Evangelical Alliance Mission

'Clive Anderson takes this little-known book and reveals to us a prophet sent by God whose purpose was to exhort and to encourage the Israelites to be patient while undergoing their oppression by the Assyrians. Every chapter shows God in control of world events, working out his purposes for the good of his people. The true church of today, under pressure from political correctness, syncretism and opposition from many quarters, would do well to ponder the encouragements mapped out in this small prophecy with a big message. Clive's portrayal of the historical backgrounds to the events found in this book, plus the questions for further study are extremely helpful.'

Rev. Peter J. Croft,
Pastor of Bethesda Baptist Church, Felixstowe, England

© Day One Publications 2005

First printed 2005

Scripture quotations are from the NIV, International Bible Society,
1973, 1978, 1984

ISBN 1 903087 74-0

9 781903 087749

British Library Cataloguing in Publication Data available

Published by Day One Publications
Ryelands Road, Leominster, HR6 8NZ
Telephone 01568 613 740   FAX 01568 611 473

email—sales@dayone.co.uk
web site—www.dayone.co.uk
North American—e-mail-sales@dayonebookstore.com
North American web site—www.dayonebookstore.com

Designed by Steve Devane and printed by Gutenberg Press, Malta

*This book is dedicated to the members of the three
churches that it has been my privilege
to serve in various capacities:*

*The Butts Evangelical Church, Alton, Hampshire
Hitherfield Road Baptist Church, Streatham, London
Lansdowne Evangelical Free Church, West Norwood,
London*

List of Bible abbreviations

THE OLD TESTAMENT		1 Chr.	1 Chronicles	Dan.	Daniel
		2 Chr.	2 Chronicles	Hosea	Hosea
Gen.	Genesis	Ezra	Ezra	Joel	Joel
Exod.	Exodus	Neh.	Nehemiah	Amos	Amos
Lev.	Leviticus	Esth.	Esther	Obad.	Obadiah
Num.	Numbers	Job	Job	Jonah	Jonah
Deut.	Deuteronomy	Ps.	Psalms	Micah	Micah
Josh.	Joshua	Prov.	Proverbs	Nahum	Nahum
Judg.	Judges	Eccles.	Ecclesiastes	Hab.	Habakkuk
Ruth	Ruth	S.of.S.	Song of Solomon	Zeph.	Zephaniah
1 Sam.	1 Samuel	Isa.	Isaiah	Hag.	Haggai
2 Sam.	2 Samuel	Jer.	Jeremiah	Zech.	Zechariah
1 Kings	1 Kings	Lam.	Lamentations	Mal.	Malachi
2 Kings	2 Kings	Ezek.	Ezekiel		

THE NEW TESTAMENT		Gal.	Galatians	Heb.	Hebrews
		Eph.	Ephesians	James	James
Matt.	Matthew	Phil.	Philippians	1 Peter	1 Peter
Mark	Mark	Col.	Colossians	2 Peter	2 Peter
Luke	Luke	1 Thes.	1 Thessalonians	1 John	1 John
John	John	2 Thes.	2 Thessalonians	2 John	2 John
Acts	Acts	1 Tim.	1 Timothy	3 John	3 John
Rom.	Romans	2 Tim.	2 Timothy	Jude	Jude
1 Cor.	1 Corinthians	Titus	Titus	Rev.	Revelation
2 Cor.	2 Corinthians	Philem.	Philemon		

Overview and Structure

Almost three thousand years ago, the ancient Assyrians began to flex their muscles. For the greater part of the period from the end of the tenth century to the seventh century BC, this dynamic military power dominated the ancient Near East. At its height the Assyrians could lay claim to an empire that stretched across Asia Minor, from Egypt in the west, to the border between Iran and India in the east, and from Russia in the north, to Arabia in the south.

At the heart of this mighty empire in its latter days lay Nineveh, encircled by massive walls and many watchtowers, guarding majestic palaces, temples and gardens. It was vast, impregnable and seemingly indestructible.

Yet the rapid collapse of mighty Nineveh is one of the great mysteries of history. So, how could Nineveh, in particular, and Assyria, in general, vanish in such a spectacular fashion? The prophet Nahum leaves us in no doubt: God was against them, but he was with his people.

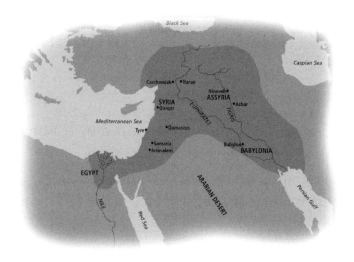

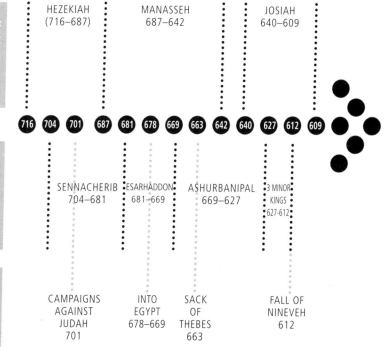

JUDAH	HEZEKIAH (716–687)	MANASSEH 687–642			JOSIAH 640–609	

716 704 701 687 681 678 669 663 642 640 627 612 609

ASSYRIA	SENNACHERIB 704–681	ESARHADDON 681–669	ASHURBANIPAL 669–627	3 MINOR KINGS 627-612

EVENTS	CAMPAIGNS AGAINST JUDAH 701	INTO EGYPT 678–669	SACK OF THEBES 663	FALL OF NINEVEH 612

OPENING UP NAHUM

Background and Summary

What possible benefits can be gained by reading a book like Nahum? The answer lies in understanding the type of literature that Nahum belongs to, and its place in the Bible and history.

Nahum the caravan

Someone once called his caravan Nahum. When asked why, he replied, 'I named my caravan Nahum because it comes after my car!' Nahum is a small, but dynamic, book in the Old Testament section of the Bible which comes after the book of Micah. It is known as one of the twelve Minor Prophets but, like the other books in that part of the Bible, it should not be considered to be of minor importance. It may be small in size but it is big in message, both for the people of Nineveh and for all who read and understand its clear warning today.

How should Nahum be understood in relation to the rest of the Bible? Each book of the Bible has a distinctive message and, when considered together, all the books reveal the big theme of the Bible: that there is salvation and blessing for all who repent, but for those who don't, there is judgement and punishment. The unfolding of biblical truth can be explained by the following: constant inspiration and progressive revelation.

Constant inspiration

The apostle Paul wrote in 2 Timothy 3:16: 'All Scripture is God-breathed and is useful for teaching, rebuking, correcting and training in righteousness, so that the man of God may be thoroughly equipped for every good work.' Some parts of the Bible may seem clearer and appear to have greater relevance to life today, but the entire Bible is intended to be read. It is a complete unit, and God through his Spirit has inspired every book and caused each one to be written and preserved for the instruction of every generation.

> Some parts of the Bible may seem clearer and appear to have greater relevance to life today, but the entire Bible is intended to be read.

Progressive revelation

This is clearly explained by Jesus in Luke 24:27: 'And beginning with Moses and all the Prophets, he explained to them what was said in all the Scriptures concerning himself.' Jesus started at the beginning, which is a very good place to start, and led them through a grand tour of the Old Testament, revealing how the great theme about himself was stated and developed in the Bible.

In addition to this, many Old Testament prophecies can be understood at three levels of understanding:

1) WHAT WAS THE ORIGINAL FULFILMENT OF THESE WORDS?

What was life like in ancient Assyria and how was this prophetic word understood by the population of that great city? So, we shall briefly interact with known Assyrian history to help to bring light and illumination to this *little-known* and *little-used* book Nahum.

2) HOW DO THEY FIND FULFILMENT IN THE EARTHLY MINISTRY OF JESUS?

According to Jesus, 'These are the Scriptures that testify about me, yet you refuse to come to me to have life' (John 5:39-40). So, what can Nahum reveal to us about him? Is there a picture, a comparison or a direct reference?

3) WHAT IS THE ULTIMATE LONG-TERM FULFILMENT OF THIS PROPHECY?

History is moving relentlessly forward to the Great Day of the Lord, and Nahum's depiction of God as Judge should enable us to gain a shadowy glimpse of the awesome events yet to come.

Also, in considering the message of this Old Testament prophet, it will be helpful to think about history and God's view of time.

Two types of history

The famous Welsh preacher of a former generation, Dr

Martyn Lloyd-Jones, said that there are two types of history: 'The history God permits and the history God promotes.' Many things take place that are beyond human comprehension but, in the permissive will of God, events are allowed to unfold. God alone has total understanding of what is happening and we are to trust in his goodness and overriding control of every situation.

Two views of time

There is intensity and brevity to time in the sight of God, as illustrated in 2 Peter 3:8.

AN INTENSITY TO TIME

'A day is like a thousand years.' This shows the seriousness of sin, for if you take one minute to sin, it appears as eight and a half months to God and, like a slow motion replay of an event, nothing is missed by God. Each word and deed is slowly drawn out and that is what makes him the perfect Judge.

A BREVITY TO TIME

'A thousand years are like a day.' He is able to see across the millennia and knows the end from the beginning, so that makes him the safest guide for any people.

History of Nineveh

Nineveh (pronounced 'Nin-evey' not 'Nin-evar') is the English biblical version of the ancient city called Ninua. It was the greatest city of the ancient Near East, being one and a half times larger than its rival Babylon and about twice as large as Rome at its greatest extent. In Jonah 3:3 we are told, 'Now Nineveh was a very important city—a visit required three days.' Since the site has been identified and partially explored, Jonah's statement has needed clarification.

Professor Donald Wiseman offers a good solution to this problem:

> The specific duration of a visit was universally recognised. As in ancient and in later Arab cultures, to make a visit involved no longer than "three days and three nights". The first day was for arrival and greeting, the second for business with the third for departure. (See also Exod. 3:18; 1 Kings 12:5,12; 1 Chr. 21:12.) Contemporary Assyrian letters are full of requests to the palace from guests arriving at a point a day's journey from Nineveh to be allowed to enter. [1]

The Assyrians were brilliant mathematicians, astronomers, engineers and warriors, yet the men from the land of Ashur struck fear and terror into many hearts. Lord Byron wrote, 'The Assyrian came down like a wolf on the fold.' To many, these people were extremely vicious. Cruelty and fear were certainly weapons in the Assyrian arsenal.

Nineveh's development

It was the great King Sennacherib (705-681 BC) who turned Nineveh into the capital city more glorious than any previously known. He spent lavishly on creating one of the wonders of the ancient world that must have been magnificent in its prime. He constructed a new city wall with eighteen gates, temples, roads, bridges, canals and a great palace which he called 'The Palace without Rival'. Sennacherib filled his new city with plazas, gardens and a large botanical and zoological park next to his palace. The citizens of Nineveh were given plots of land on which to plant orchards. Esarhaddon, his son, built the main arsenal at Nineveh, and also a palace on the mound that is now called Nebu Yunus (mound of Jonah). Any plans he had for more development ended when he died on the way to a campaign in Egypt.

His son, Ashurbanipal, (669-626 BC) became the last great king of Assyria and to him we owe a debt for the great library of his which was discovered at Nineveh. [2]

You are the weakest link. Goodbye.

Nineveh's power waned dramatically and its end came in August 612 BC when it was mercilessly sacked and laid waste by the coalition armies of the Babylonians and the Medes. Its destruction was so complete that for almost one thousand five hundred years its exact location remained a mystery. Sceptics sneered at tales about Nineveh, and treated it, along with the book of Jonah, as a mere legend that belonged to an age of fantastic tales and fables.

> Its destruction was so complete that for almost one thousand five hundred years its exact location remained a mystery.

It was almost by accident that Austin Henry Layard (pronounced Laird) came upon the ancient ruins, although another Assyriologist, Paolo Emilio Botta, would be the first definitely to identify the site. In 1846 Layard's rediscovery of Nineveh became front-page news in the papers of the British Empire, and, subsequently, many of its monuments found their way into the great museums of the world. Indeed, one discovery—the wall reliefs depicting the siege and defeat of the Israelite city of Lachish—hit the headlines, for here was the first corroboration of an event mentioned in the Bible (see 2 Kings 18:17).

> Nahum is, therefore, not just a caravan—something used occasionally. Here is a vital book and a message that speaks powerfully to every age.

Sir Stratford Canning, the Ambassador to the Turkish capital in Constantinople, wrote to Layard about the excitement generated by his discoveries, saying, 'What I would not give to be with you; my curiosity is not only on tiptoe, but on stilts.'

A word of caution

One danger that must be avoided is that of seeking to apply twenty-first century society's values and experiences to previous generations. It can be forgotten that many items which are so commonplace now, were just not available even relatively recently in the earth's history. By way of contrast though, God's Word is timeless and speaks powerfully to each generation.

Nahum is, therefore, not just a caravan—something used occasionally. Here is a vital book and a message that speaks powerfully to every age. As it says later on in the Bible, 'He who has an ear, let him hear what the Spirit says…' (Rev. 2:7).

For further study ▶

FOR FURTHER STUDY

1. Read Romans 15:4 and 1 Corinthians 10:11 to see the apostle Paul's valuation of the Old Testament.

2. How often do the words 'Lord' or 'God' appear in Nahum, and in what context are they used?

3. Many Christians believe that it is God who is speaking when the Bible is read. Do you agree with this statement and would you be able to show others why you believe it to be true?

TO THINK ABOUT AND DISCUSS

1. If ancient history has no appeal for you, will it stop you from reading the Old Testament section of the Bible?

2. When it comes to reading or studying any book of the Bible, does length matter?

3. Today the ruined site of ancient Nineveh is located across the River Tigris, opposite Mosul in Northern Iraq. Does this fact help to make a study of Nahum more relevant to you?

4. Many today reject traditional dating schemes and no longer use BC (Before Christ) and AD (Anno Domini), meaning in the year of our Lord. Instead, museums and archaeological sites use BCE (Before Common Era) and CE (Common Era). What do you think this tells us about people's attitudes to Jesus Christ and Christianity?

1 God's burden is revealed

(1:1-3a)

In his infinite mercy God always reveals himself and his ways before he demonstrates his power. All are without excuse because the created order, his Word and his Son proclaim that there is a God over all who is to be worshipped, loved and obeyed.

God's oracle (v. 1a)

An oracle indicates that this is a message that has been given by God. Some translators prefer the word 'burden' to oracle, as it focuses the mind more emphatically on the problem that there was in the world at that time, and so it became a burden in the heart of God's prophet. It is a weighty message for it tells of impending disaster and doom if repentance is not forthcoming in the hearts of the Ninevites.

Are you serious?

The focus of the burden is the great capital city of the Assyrians. It would have seemed incredible to those who first heard this message and many, no doubt, would have thought this was either the prediction of the sadly disillusioned, or the ranting of a deranged mind. Those living in the west of the empire would not have considered that these few words offered much hope, for the nation of Judah was feeling alone and isolated. The northern kingdom of Israel had previously been taken into exile by the Assyrians; Judah, the southern kingdom, awaited the same fate to befall it.

Yet the burden of Nineveh was its impending doom, not Judah's; and it was based not on logic or tactics but on the power and fulfilment of God's word.

Predicting the future

The ancient Assyrians had an elaborate system for trying to discover the will of the gods. Exorcists and diviners played a great part in daily life, and many of these experts would have been trained at Babylon or by someone schooled in the Babylonian way of doing things.

The idea behind divination was that the gods would communicate their intentions and preferences by leaving hidden clues that could only be read and understood by a specialist. Depending on the situation and available material, the exorcists or diviners would consult the stars or celestial phenomena, the pattern of smoke from burning incense, the behaviour of birds and other animals, and the liver or entrails of specially selected animals, normally lambs or sheep. Clay models were produced to teach trainees what marks to look out for. In Ezekiel 21:21 there is the account of the Babylonian king, Nebuchadnezzar, seeking an omen and consulting the sheep's liver before deciding which city to attack. The gods would be invited to reveal their requirements within the body of a specific animal and after it was slaughtered, it would be examined by the experts who had spent many years learning how to read the gods' writing. Thankfully, Almighty God communicates in a simple fashion. He uses words transmitted by the written or the spoken word.

God speaks about the future (v. 1b)

The messenger that God chose to deliver this prophetic word was Nahum the Elkoshite, who has remained a mystery to succeeding generations; no one knows who he was or even the location of his home town, Elkosh. A number of sites has been suggested but none has found universal acceptance.

Capernaum, located on the north-west shore of Lake Galilee, is or near the location that archaeologists are looking for. The name Capernaum means 'village of Nahum'. If there is a connection, it would be most appropriate. Jesus came here after leaving Nazareth and in Mark 2:1 there is that noteworthy sentence, 'A few days later, when Jesus again entered Capernaum, the people heard that he had come *home*' (italics mine). Here he called Matthew to follow him. Here he taught and preached, and did many great works. But he also predicted Capernaum's downfall and today it is just a tourist site, with a number of interesting remains to see. So there could be a link between Nahum foretelling the downfall of Nineveh and the Great Prophet, the Lord Jesus Christ, inferring that they should remember Nahum, otherwise a like judgement would come upon the people and place of Capernaum.

Comfort? Are you sure?

Nahum's name means comfort, even though his prophecy contains many vivid scenes of judgement and destruction. Yet he was a comfort to those who were going to have the threat of Nineveh removed for ever and he is able to help all who subsequently read his book for he reveals that God is in control.

Sin brings alienation in life, often from those who would be the greatest help and comfort. Is it not a strange thing that Nineveh's later kings had sought to destroy the people from whom Jonah had come? Even though his was a word of judgement, by believing it the people and the city had been saved. Now, a new messenger is sent who brings comfort, not to the Ninevites, but to the people of Judah.

> God is totally different from us. He alone creates, sustains and controls everything that exists.

God is jealous (v. 2)

God is totally different from us. He alone creates, sustains and controls everything that exists. We must not project on to him human characteristics, unless the Bible gives us the licence to do so. So, when Nahum wrote that God is jealous and avenges himself, he was speaking of the perfect way that God acts and he was not describing the rash behaviour of humanity. In speaking of God as jealous, Nahum is not saying that God is:

CAPRICIOUS—he does not have any unreasonable change of mind or character;

MALICIOUS—he is not spiteful;

VICIOUS—he is not cruel.

God alone is holy and pure, and works all things in accordance with his unchanging nature, as it is recorded in Genesis 18:25: 'Will not the Judge of all the earth do right?'

God will punish sin (v. 3a)

God's character is revealed in the way he acts in time and space.

God's jealousy is long-suffering

Ever since Adam and Eve disobeyed him, God has been long-suffering in his treatment of sinners. When he came to Adam in Genesis 3:19, God said to him, 'For dust you are and to dust you will return.' But it did not happen immediately. God was long-suffering in his treatment

> God alone is holy and pure, and works all things in accordance with his unchanging nature, as it is recorded in Genesis 18:25: 'Will not the Judge of all the earth do right?'

of Adam and he certainly was in his handling of Nineveh. Jonah had witnessed that fact even though it caused him to sulk (see Jonah 4:1-4). God's delay in executing punishment is not a sign of weakness. Mercy can be misinterpreted as a failing. But to follow that line of reasoning is an act of folly because a stay of execution does not mean that the threat has been lifted. Each generation also receives due warning through the Bible about God and his judgements. May we not be taken unawares, especially when the end of all things finally comes.

God's delay is not a remission of punishment

The clear message of the Bible is that God does punish sin. Although it may be some time before he does, it will happen. Paul wrote in 2 Thessalonians 1:7b-9, '...when the Lord Jesus is revealed from heaven in blazing fire with his powerful angels. He will punish those who do not know God and do not obey the gospel of our Lord Jesus. They will be punished with everlasting destruction and shut out from the presence of the Lord and from the majesty of his power.'

Nineveh was going to receive the judgement that had been postponed at the time of Jonah. God did not judge the city then, but it did not mean that he would ignore the sins of subsequent generations—far from it! Past blessing does not guarantee present peace. The people of each generation must seek and serve God for themselves.

God's jealousy is often provoked to vengeance

It is not just in the life to come that God deals justly with people; he will also do so in this life. Described here is the simple idea of definite punishment. Only, it must be remembered that divine punishment is retribution and not retaliation. Sin will receive its just punishment, and the unrepentant sinner will not be able to escape the sentence that God delivers. God's jealousy has not only the warmth of his love but also the fire of his wrath.

> It is not just in the life to come that God deals justly with people; he will also do so in this life.

In C. S. Lewis's book, *The Lion, the Witch and the Wardrobe*, the children, Peter, Susan and Lucy, are told by the Beavers about Aslan.

Susan asks, 'Who is Aslan?'

Mr Beaver replies, 'Aslan is a lion—*the* Lion, the great Lion.'

Susan then says, 'Is he—quite safe?'

'Safe?' said Mr Beaver. 'Who said anything about safe? 'Course he isn't safe. But he's good. He's the King, I tell you.'

That, in story form, is what the Bible clearly teaches about Almighty God.

Nothing to worry about?

God is not out of touch with the world but intimately interested in it. So much so, that his one and only Son became

> If repentance for sin does not take place and the free offer of salvation and life is not accepted, then, instead of experiencing the warmth of God's love, we shall be the recipients for evermore of the fire of his wrath.

a human being. Jesus bore his people's sin in his body on the cross; he suffered the full force of God's vengeance. But if repentance for sin does not take place and the free offer of salvation and life is not accepted, then, instead of experiencing the warmth of God's love, we shall be the recipients for evermore of the fire of his wrath.

FOR FURTHER STUDY

1. What view of creation do Psalm 19:1-6 and Romans 1:18-20 present? Why is it that most people do not view the creation in this way?

2. Paul describes the wages of sin in Romans 6:23a. Why are the wages of sin so drastic and final and what does that verse tell us about God's view of sin?

3. In the Lord Jesus Christ, God has shown his great love and his unswerving determination to punish sin. What does this tell us about the character of God? Read John 3:14-21.

TO THINK ABOUT AND DISCUSS

1. Nahum was unknown, yet he was the mouthpiece of God. In our celebrity- driven age, is it a problem for us, as Christians, to remain in the background so that God's Word can be heard or do we long to be in a position of prominence?

2. In certain situations it is sometimes said, 'You have to be cruel to be kind.' Is it hard for us to understand that a message of comfort can also be one that brings judgement on God's enemies?

3. Nahum's message seems to be irrelevant to many today. Is there a way that you could show others that it is not outdated, but of great importance for all people?

4. How would you, as a Christian, respond to a neighbour who informs you that he or she is using a fortune-teller for guidance?

2 God's power is clearly seen

(1:3b-6)

Nahum should not be misunderstood. He did not have a primitive view of the forces of nature being an expression of the gods' pleasure or displeasure. He knew enough theology to avoid making such a simple mistake. The one true God is above and beyond the created order, but he does control it and has used the elements in the past to bring judgement on the earth.

A number of scenarios are now put before the inhabitants of Nineveh and they are in the form of rhetorical questions because God knows that they already know the answer to these things. But he wants them to hear and reflect on past events recorded in the Bible and, by implication, known throughout the ancient Near East at that time.

Weather report (v. 3b)

The first great event alluded to here is surely the great

worldwide Flood connected with Noah and his family, an event that has found its way into every culture on earth. It was recorded by the ancient Babylonians and would have been well known by the people of Nineveh.

The great lesson they were to learn from this was that, although Assyria and her warriors might bring terror and fright throughout the ancient Near East, the greatest warrior of all, God himself, was against them. He has a frightening array of weapons in his arsenal, and nothing that any person can invent will ever rival his eternal power.

The terrifying powers of the earth's atmosphere are under his authority and God uses them to bring justice to this world of sin and shame. When Noah stood against the wickedness of his generation, God gave a mighty demonstration of power. Proud men thought they were in total control, but had all their hopes and dreams shattered as they perished in the water.

> God ... has a frightening array of weapons in his arsenal, and nothing that any person can invent will ever rival his eternal power.

In the book of Genesis information is given about the state of the earth before the flood waters came. The Bible is not primarily a scientific document but when it touches on these things it does so with unerring accuracy. One vital piece of data is contained in Genesis 2:6: 'Streams came up from the earth and watered the whole surface of the ground.' This means that it had never rained before the Flood came upon the earth and, across the globe, similar temperatures would have been experienced. That is why fossil records are so similar over the whole earth, including the remains of dinosaurs, which have been found in just about every place in the world, including regions that could not sustain such life today. So when Noah, under God, started to say, 'It's going to rain.'

'What's rain?' would have been the response.

Perhaps, as time wore on, Noah was dismissed as just an old crank. But the day came when God sent all the animals into the ark, along with Noah's family. Did the watching world wonder at this spectacle? Did they laugh? Well, whatever their reaction, God then did something that had never happened before. Instead of streams coming up to water the earth, the rain started to fall. What then of the sneers and the jibes and jokes? All unbelief was swept away as the pools developed into lakes, and the lakes into one vast sea that covered the whole earth.

> All unbelief was swept away as the pools developed into lakes, and the lakes into one vast sea that covered the whole earth.

To paraphrase it, it was as if Nahum were saying, 'People of Nineveh, don't say that Nahum's warning is hollow just because God did not blow you away at the time of Jonah. It does not mean that he will not carry out the threat of his judgement this time. Consider the length of time it took to complete the ark, but then the rain did fall.'

Nahum now moves on and refers to another mighty event in the earth's history.

They did not walk on water (v. 4)

The Hebrew people were trapped and we can imagine how terrified they must have been. Exodus records the unfolding drama and leaves us in no doubt as to the perilous situation facing the Hebrew people. In Exodus 14:12, the people reacted hopelessly and they wanted to go back to Egypt, to the land of bondage. Moses responded in verse 13 by saying, 'Stand firm.' But God, whom no one seems to have bothered to ask, speaks out and says, in verse 15, 'Move on!' This is a brilliant cameo of the Christian life. Too often when difficulties arise, we want to go back. Others may tell us to stand firm, but God wants us to move on in faith placing our reliance upon him. To show God was in total control, Moses was commanded to stretch out his hand. The sea parted and they crossed over, every last one of them, on dry land.

> 'Move on!' This is a brilliant cameo of the Christian life. Too often when difficulties arise, we want to go back. Others may tell us to stand firm, but God wants us to move on in faith placing our reliance upon him.

To paraphrase again, 'People of Nineveh, beware! You may feel that you are like Pharaoh's army—strong, invincible—and you have God's people just where you want them. But remember Pharaoh's mistake. He forgot about God and it cost him dear. Are you, too, going to make the same mistake?'

Yet more water

When the people were going into the Promised Land, God dried up the Jordan River so that the multitudes could enter the land he was giving them. When referring to this, Joshua, the leader who succeeded Moses, said, 'The LORD will do amazing things among you' (Josh. 3:5).

Travellers today can wonder what was so amazing about the events recorded in Joshua 3, for when visiting the Jordan River near Jericho, the river appears small and relatively narrow. That is because a great volume of water is drained off to irrigate both Israel and Jordan so that the Dead Sea into which the Jordan River flows has receding banks and is in very real danger of drying up, thereby giving a false impression of its former size and strength. However, in the time of Joshua, it was wider, and crossing it could be a treacherous affair.

A deliberate parallel is made here with Nineveh, as it relied on the protection and provision given to it by the River Tigris. But that natural barrier would not stop the judgement of God taking place.

Too good to change?

Even the lovely areas that provide beauty and sustenance are not beyond his control and the challenge is thrown down here: 'In what do you put your trust?' Whatever it is can be removed and you will find yourself bereft of help and life itself. Bashan stands for rich pasture, which was coveted by many surrounding nations. Carmel was a region that was full of cornfields and was crucially important to the sustenance of the economy, as well as providing food supplies. Lebanon, with its forests and its famed cedars, was an area rich in produce and was potential for any controlling power. All of these areas had come into the Assyrian Empire when Israel fell in 722 BC, but they were going to be devastated by God and there was nothing the Assyrians could do to stop him acting against them.

The earth moved for them (vv. 5-6)

Genesis 13 describes the area around the Dead Sea as being very beautiful and fruitful, so much so that when Abraham and Lot came to separate, 'Lot looked up and saw that the whole plain of the Jordan was well watered, like the garden of the LORD, like the land of Egypt, towards Zoar' (Gen. 13:10). But the outward beauty could not mask the inward corruption and decadence of the inhabitants of that region and the anger of God was going to be unleashed against them. Abraham did all he could to act as mediator for them, pleading with God for mercy, as recorded in Genesis 18:16-33.

Yet ten people could not be found who loved or followed the Lord. Lot, however, was given the chance to escape with his family before judgement fell. He hesitated and had to be pulled by the angels sent to rescue him and after staggering into a place of refuge, the town of Zoar, God acted in judgement. The heavens rained down sulphur. So complete was the devastation that the cities of the plain just disappeared from history. They have been considered by

> These historical references should not lull anyone into a false sense of security, for the Bible is always forward looking... Whatever has happened in the past will pale into insignificance when Jesus comes again. History records God's dealings in the past and the Bible points to God's dealings in the future.

many to be just another ancient myth, rather like Nineveh before its rediscovery.

Is history dry as dust?

These historical references should not lull anyone into a false sense of security, for the Bible is always forward looking. Therefore, do not become complacent. Whatever has happened in the past will pale into insignificance when Jesus comes again.

History records God's dealings in the past and the Bible points to God's dealings in the future.

Nineveh did not believe God and his word. Are we in danger of making the same mistake?

FOR FURTHER STUDY

1. In Genesis 19:23-28 there is a devastating account of God's judgement being unleashed. Does this seem to run contrary to the Bible's statements about God being a God of love?

2. See Isaiah 30:30-32 for a prophecy concerning the use of the elements against Assyria. Do you think that God acts in the same way today against the nations of the world?

3. Then read Ezekiel 47:7-12 to see how that area, which was severely judged, will one day be a place of blessing and fruitfulness. Does this give us any hope for the future of creation?

TO THINK ABOUT AND DISCUSS

1. Can you think of any other Old Testament examples where God gives people a warning before his judgement falls on them?

2. In our modern culture, what significance should we place on looking back into history for lessons or examples from which to learn?

3. The Dead Sea is in danger of disappearing altogether. Are there other environmental areas of concern that you can think of? What should be the Christian's response to the destruction of natural resources?

4. Read Hebrews 12:25-29 and discuss how the meaning of the word 'shake' might apply today.

3 God's patience is explained

(1:7-8)

God reveals his constant love towards his people and his patience towards his enemies. That is why he permits evil in the world. However, time will run out for the wicked.

God is with his people (v. 7)

The great nineteenth-century preacher, Charles Haddon Spurgeon, said, 'Have you read this chapter through? It is a very terrible one; it is like the rushing of a mighty river when it is nearing a cataract. It boils and seethes and flows with overwhelming force, bearing everything before it; yet right in the middle of the surging flood, stands out, like a green island, this most cheering, comforting and delightful text.'

What an oasis of peace it is for the uniqueness of God is revealed here. All people are good some of the time, but he, the Lord Almighty, is good all of the time, as the hymn writer said:

How good is the God we adore,
Our faithful, unchangeable friend,
Whose love is as great as his power
and knows neither measure nor end. [1]

God's people were rightly fearful. But, in the past, the city of Nineveh had seen the goodness of God on display when he sent the reluctant preacher, Jonah, to them. So none of them could ever accuse him of being unfair now because he had been gracious in the past. The Ninevites had responded to Jonah's message with repentance and that had brought salvation and blessing to them because God did not destroy them. Tragically, they had forgotten his mercy. Trouble was coming their way and the only way of escape was by seeking safety in the presence of the one true God.

Reminding the people of past events, Nahum says, 'The LORD is good', and many people should be able to acknowledge that fact. He then goes on to describe the positive benefit from a living relationship with God.

> Here, God is compared by Nahum to a refuge. When people come to him, they find that he is the one who cares for them, not just in their lifetime, but also through death and on into eternity.

A refuge required

God is referred to here in a way that the ancient people could readily understand as a 'refuge in times of trouble'. There were no early warning systems, or ground-to-air missiles to give protection to the population at large. They needed to be in a safe place. Safe cities were specifically designed to cater for large numbers who could take refuge when an enemy was advancing on their land. Here, God is compared by Nahum to a refuge. When people come to him, they find that he is the one who cares for them, not just in their lifetime, but also through death and on into eternity.

The ultimate example of this is the Lord Jesus who, on one occasion, was challenged by the Jews to prove that he really was the Christ. He used a simple, but profound, illustration to impress upon them that he is God. He said about his people, 'I give them eternal life, and they shall never perish; no one can snatch them out of my hand. My Father, who has given them to me, is greater than all; no one can snatch them out of my Father's hand.' Then he probably brought his hands together in a firm clench and said, 'I and the Father are one' (John 10:28-30). That is the ultimate refuge, locked into God's hands, safe and secure, never to slip or fall.

> That is the ultimate refuge, locked into God's hands, safe and secure, never to slip or fall.

It was as if Nahum were saying, 'Nineveh, to the world at large, you may appear big brash and brave, but nothing compares to having God as Lord and Saviour, and his covenant people are to rejoice in this great fact.'

The result of faith

Nineveh is reminded that God is the ultimate carer: 'He cares for those who trust in him.' He shows grace to all people but especially to those who have put their trust in him. (For a more in-depth study of this great subject see *Grace—amazing grace* by Brian Edwards.) But there is a great warning issued here for his love will not overlook sin; and to be true to himself, God must punish sin. This is what Nahum sets alongside the grace of God.

> But there is a great warning issued here for his love will not overlook sin; and to be true to himself, God must punish sin.

God is against his enemies (v. 8)

God will punish them in ways that they can clearly understand. Nineveh had the River Tigris as a natural barrier on its eastern side, and a branch of that river would be used to bring judgement upon them. God often uses what is considered to be protection or insurance against a rainy day to judge people. So will it be here.

Remember Noah and Lot

It has been said that the best form of teaching is repetition. Teach people what they need to know and then teach it to them all over again. So, here is another reminder to the inhabitants. The ancient people of that region knew all about the great Flood. On display in the British Museum in London are two accounts of this event. They are the Atrahasis and the Gilgamesh Epics. In each a different name is given to the central character of those stories: Atrahasis and Utnapishtim respectively. There are many significant differences when compared with the account in Genesis but there is no doubt that this event had left its mark on the history of that area.

It is a serious thing to contemplate, but out of all the population on earth at the time, only Noah and his family were saved. Also, Lot just made it in time into the city of safety. But all those people in Sodom and Gomorrah perished, not in a torrent of water, but of sulphur, rained down and many perished as God pursued them into darkness. Therefore, Nineveh was also to learn these great lessons from history.

Jesus too clearly warned people that if they die without crying to God for forgiveness, they too would go into outer darkness (Matt. 8:12; 22:13).

> He never has to justify his actions to anyone but God graciously condescends to reveal to the Ninevites that he is against them.

God is alive and active on planet earth

He never has to justify his actions to anyone but God graciously condescends to reveal to the Ninevites that he is against them. The great name of God, shown in Hebrew by four letters, YHWH, occurs three times in verse 2, three times in the following six verses and is connected here with his judgement. This is in a form of parallelism.

A GREAT PROCLAMATION—THE CHARACTER OF GOD (V. 2)

i)   The LORD is a jealous and avenging God;

ii)   The LORD takes vengeance and is filled with wrath.

iii) The LORD takes vengeance on his foes and maintains his wrath against his enemies.

A GREAT EXPLANATION—THE ACTIVITY OF GOD (VV. 3,8)

i)   The LORD is slow to anger and great in power (v. 3);

ii)   The LORD will not leave the guilty unpunished (v. 3).

iii) The LORD is good, a refuge in times of trouble. He cares for those who trust in him, but with an overwhelming flood he will make an end of Nineveh (vv. 7-8).

For believers, the name of Jesus is very precious. How grateful they are that he has been revealed to them. John Newton brilliantly summed up the believer's love in the following hymn:

How sweet the name of Jesus sounds
In a believer's ear!
It soothes his sorrows, heals his wounds,
And drives away his fear.

It makes the wounded spirit whole,
And calms the troubled breast;
It's manna to the hungry soul,
And to the weary rest.

Dear name! the rock on which I build,
My shield and hiding-place;

My never-failing treasury filled
With boundless stores of grace.

Through you my prayers acceptance gain,
Although with sin defiled;
Satan accuses me in vain,
And I am owned a child.

Jesus! My Shepherd, Husband, Friend,
My Prophet, Priest, and King;
My Lord, my Life, my Way, my End,
Accept the praise I bring.

Weak is the effort of my heart,
And cold my warmest thought;
But when I see you as you are,
I'll praise you as I should.

Till then I would your love proclaim,
With every fleeting breath;
And may the music of your name
Refresh my soul in death. [2]

FOR FURTHER STUDY

1. In Luke 16:19-31 Jesus gives teaching about the reality of the life to come. Some think this is a parable but parables use anonymous characters. Jesus here deliberately uses a name. Did he want people to think about someone they had known called Lazarus and was he saying to them, 'Now I will tell you what happened to him and what may also happen to you'?

2. Psalm 23 contains wonderful statements about the eternal security of the Christian. How many of the word pictures are based on reality and what other parts of the Bible speak about the same things?

TO THINK ABOUT AND DISCUSS

1. Nahum sets God's goodness and justice alongside each other as two aspects of his character. Is this true to the rest of the Bible?

2. Many people think that the whole idea of the Bible's teaching on hell and eternal punishment is either a sick joke or literary licence to encourage obedience. Does verse 8 help you to understand this teaching in the Bible and could you use it to help others to think about this difficult subject?

3. In John chapter 10 Jesus describes simply, yet vividly, the security of the Christian believer. After reading this chapter, do you think that Jesus is describing the only way to lasting peace or are there other ways to God?

4 God's proclamation about Nineveh

(1:9-14)

Many years earlier the people of Nineveh had responded to Jonah's preaching, but now they were insensitive to the voice of God. Today, many look for meaning but refuse to consider that the God of the Bible has any relevance for their lives.

Resistance to God is futile (vv. 9-10)

The prophet Jeremiah said, 'The heart is deceitful above all things and beyond cure. Who can understand it?' (17:9). He wrote those words to a people who did not learn the Assyrian lesson and just a few years later the mighty armies of the Babylonian king, Nebuchadnezzar (who had been at the final collapse of Nineveh), took the people of Judah into exile.

So Nahum warns the Ninevites before that time that no amount of human ingenuity will be an adequate barrier against God's power. Their hearts planned many schemes to thwart the will of God. But he knows the human heart and we are no match for him.

Had Jonah brought a revival to Nineveh?

Revival has been described as a 'people saturated with God'. [1] It is a time when God moves among his people and motivates them in a way that makes an impact on society through the preaching of God's Word and the holy lives of his people so that many are challenged and changed for good by God's grace.

> Nahum warns the Ninevites before that time that no amount of human ingenuity will be an adequate barrier against God's power.

The book of Jonah does not speak of a great revival—a turning to God in repentance and faith that lasted. The Ninevites do not appear to be a people saturated with God. Although Jesus did say in Matthew 12:41, 'The men of Nineveh will stand up at the judgement with this generation and condemn it; for they repented at the preaching of Jonah, and now one greater than Jonah is here.' He was speaking about a short, not a long-term, turning to God. They did repent initially but the change was not lasting, for Assyrian history does not show a great or lasting effect as a result of Jonah's reluctant preaching.

According to 2 Kings 14:25 Jonah prophesied during the reign of Jeroboam II, (c. 782-753 BC), when the king on the throne at Nineveh was Ashur-Dan III, (772-754 BC). He had begun a period of conquest, and it was probably after one campaign that Jonah arrived. Following him was Ashur-Nirari V, (754-744 BC), and then came the warrior, Tiglath-Pileser III, who campaigned against Israel and started the deportation programme that was completed by his son, Shalmaneser V. The ten tribes were absorbed into the empire, never to return.

So it did not take long for the warlike qualities to come to the forefront again, and Jonah and his message were soon forgotten as they set off conquering other people groups.

> So it did not take long for the warlike qualities to come to the forefront again, and Jonah and his message were soon forgotten as they set off conquering other people groups.

How similar this was to the children of Israel in the Old Testament as they wandered through the wilderness. Time and again they incurred the severe displeasure of the Lord and then there was a turning to him in repentance when he acted against them. But it had no lasting effect and they again incurred his severest displeasure. The writer to the Hebrews uses this to telling effect when he says, 'Today, if you hear his voice, do not harden your hearts as you did in the rebellion' (Heb. 3:15).

The repentance shown as a result of Jonah's preaching cannot be put in the same category as the Great Awakening of the eighteenth century, when under the preaching of George Whitefield, John Wesley and others a great work of God took place that had long-lasting benefits. All too quickly the Ninevites reverted to type and they were now going to be called to account for thinking that they were masters of their own destiny. This is carefully explained to them. Thomas Brooks notes:

> True penitential confession is joined with reformation. He that does not forsake his sin, as well as confess it, forsakes the benefit of his confession. And indeed, there is no real confession of sin, where there is no real forsaking of sin. It is not enough for us to confess the sins we have committed, but we must resolve against committing again the sins we have committed.[2]

Audacious resistance to him is wrong (v. 11)

At that time all the peoples of the ancient Near East feared the unconquerable armies of the Assyrians. They had displayed an arrogance which is often the parent of both daring and cruelty, and like many others who dominate the frail, they became contemptuous of the weak. At the head of this empire in Nineveh was one who not only despised others but also dared to confront and take on Almighty God: he 'plots evil against the LORD'.

There are a number of writers who think that this is a reference to King Sennacherib who came against Judah in his campaign of 701 BC and who was a particular threat to Jerusalem. However, history, both biblical and secular, tells how he failed to take Jerusalem, even though he recorded on the Taylor Prism that is now in the British Museum 'He (King Hezekiah) himself I shut up in Jerusalem, his royal city, like a bird in a cage. I surrounded him with watchposts and made it impossible for anyone to go in or out of his city.' Yet Sennacherib did not have the key to the cage so he went back to Nineveh a defeated man, for the Bible says that God's angel inflicted heavy casualties on his army (Isaiah 37:36-37) and he died in 681 BC. He was succeeded by his son, Esarhaddon, who reigned from 681-669 BC.

So who are you talking about, Nahum?

Nahum gives us a clue as to whom he is referring to by mentioning the overthrow of Thebes in Egypt in Nahum 3:8-11. This took place in 663 BC and Nahum prophesied after that time and before the fall of Nineveh in 612 BC. The action against Thebes was carried out by the last great king of Assyria, Ashurbanipal, (669-627 BC), who was the son and successor of Esarhaddon. As his records show, he was not only a scholarly man but a ruthless leader of the army and an implacable enemy to many. This was the man Nahum spoke about.

God redeems his people (vv. 12-13)

The little nation of Judah was saved because God had moved against her enemies. He was for them because they were his people. The Bible gives the highest possible place to God, and, in describing him and his activity, a number of fundamental, yet staggering, things about him are revealed. This helps us to understand that trying to resist him is wrong.

GOD IS OMNISCIENT—he knows everything (Ps. 147:5).
GOD IS OMNIPRESENT—he is everywhere (Ps. 139).
GOD IS OMNIPOTENT—he is all powerful (Job 42:2; Matt. 19:26).
For he cannot be stopped in his tracks or distracted from his purpose.

Safety in numbers?

> God's action against the allies is comprehensive and decisive: 'Cut off and pass away.'

There were many against the one, but Assyrian allies could not stop the hand of God from saving the people of Judah or carrying out his plan against Nineveh. God's action against the allies is comprehensive and decisive: 'Cut off and pass away.'

These things the Ninevites would have known from their encounter with Jonah about 130 years before and from Sennacherib's defeat outside Jerusalem in 701BC, just eighty-nine years before the fall of Nineveh.

This brings great comfort to the covenant people of God. Although life may become extremely difficult, God will not leave or forsake those who are his. His eternal promise stands sure. He may discipline his children but he will bring them to life and joy everlasting. That is the sure hope set before the believer.

God guards his people (v. 14)

Even though our senses may sometimes lead us to think otherwise, God is always for his people. He may, like a wise parent, discipline the unwary or foolish, but he never stops loving them.

One of the great object lessons of the Bible is given in Isaiah 44, where the prophet speaks of the futile and pathetic nature of idols. Speaking of a tree, he says that some of it is taken and shaped into a figure that is then venerated and the other bit is used as fuel for the fire.

> Although life may become extremely difficult, God will not leave or forsake those who are his ... Even though our senses may sometimes lead us to think otherwise, God is always for his people.

The Assyrians were no different. There are many fascinating books about their beliefs but they show that it is difficult to try and recreate Nineveh's temples and shrines. Concerning the place where Sennacherib was slain, 'the temple of his god Nisroch' (2 Kings 19:37), Jeremy Black and Anthony Green write, 'It is not clear to which Assyrian god this refers; it has been suggested that it is a corruption of Ninurta, but this is unsubstantiated.'

When Nineveh fell, the temples were filled with the slaughter of many penitents crying out for help to the deities these temples represented. But instead of relief, the houses of their gods became their tombs. It is a sad fact that down the centuries many have perished in places they have fled to for refuge.

False gods all pass away. But the one true and eternal God will never be irrelevant or forgotten. He lives for ever, and he will not give his glory to any other.

Yet the history of the world since the Fall in the Garden of Eden shows all too clearly how people's minds have been warped and they have done any number of foolish things to satisfy the desire to worship.

The one true and eternal God will never be irrelevant or forgotten. He lives for ever, and he will not give his glory to any other.

For further study ▶

FOR FURTHER STUDY

1. In Jonah 4 we see just how reluctant Jonah was about preaching to the people of Nineveh. Can you think of other examples in the Bible where people were reluctant to be God's spokesmen?

2. Why did Jesus use Jonah as an example of his own ministry? Read Matthew 12:38-45 to put Jesus' teaching about Jonah into context.

3. Isaiah 44:6-23 is a brilliant display of the stupidity of idol worship. Read it through a couple of times to gain a sense of the full impact of his words and then consider how you might write them for today's generation.

TO THINK ABOUT AND DISCUSS

1. Many forget how fragile and unpredictable life can be. Are there any clues in what you have just read to suggest why ignoring God's will for our lives is a very dangerous thing to do?

2. How many examples can you give of people deliberately ignoring God today while thinking that he will receive them into heaven when they die?

3. The Bible tells us that God is a Spirit (John 4:24). As we cannot see him, do you think this is a big factor in people considering him to be irrelevant, a case of being out of sight and out of mind? How, as a Christian, could you teach them the foolishness of this position?

4. What sort of idols do people have today? Should the choice be limited to Isaiah's example of a piece of timber?

5 God guarantees his people's protection

(1:15)

It is sad to think how often Christian people forget that God has given them great and precious promises (2 Peter 1:4). Not only are these promises given to encourage but also to uphold the believer in times of fear and danger.

God's deliverance is clearly stated (v. 15a)

The city of Jerusalem is elevated, situated high up in the Judean hills, as Psalm 122:4 makes clear: 'That is where the tribes go up.' So it is that the people are to look for the herald, the messenger who brings news that will thrill and delight their hearts, and they are to look for this message to be delivered soon. If we had been living in Judea at this time, we too might have found these words too incredible to believe. But the deliverance that God promises will come, for God always keeps his promises.

The pilgrim's story

In *The Pilgrim's Progress*, Part I, by John Bunyan, Christian and Hopeful have left God's pathway to go their own way. At first, this seemed to be a better way than God's, but they became lulled into a false sense of security and as a result were locked up in the dungeon of Doubting Castle by Giant Despair. Bunyan brilliantly shows how doubt and despair often go hand in hand when God's Word is forgotten or not believed and the ensuing problems that arise from that situation.

Eventually Christian remembers what he should have never forgotten. 'What a fool! What a fool I am to lie here in this stinking dungeon when I might walk free on the highway to glory! I have a key close to my heart called promise which I am sure will open any door in Doubting Castle. So it was when he applied the key, they were free and the fearful Giant Despair could not restrain them.' [1]

> If we are born-again believers, then we should avail ourselves of God's very great and precious promises. They are the Christian's birthright and possession.

The people in Judah, particularly in Jerusalem, should have remembered the great promises of God. The message may be stated like this: 'Have you forgotten how in 701 BC the formidable army of Sennacherib surrounded your walls, and how, through the words of the prophet Isaiah, you were told not to despair or doubt because the enemy would not gain entry and defeat you? Isaiah may not be around but God is still the same. His messenger may be different but his message is still the same. So give to Nahum the same respect you gave to Isaiah and listen to what he says, so that you may not be held by the giant of despair in the castle of doubt. '

If we are born-again believers, then we should avail ourselves of God's very great and precious promises. They are the Christian's birthright and possession.

God's deliverance must be faithfully preached (v. 15b)

If the good news is to be believed then it has to be communicated authentically and clearly, for when God's Word is taught then his voice is heard. God the Holy Spirit takes the Word of God to produce the people of God. That is why clarity in communication is so important.

One of the great benefits of the Christian community gathering regularly together is that of encouraging one another in the faith. True Christian fellowship is wonderful and should be highly prized and sought after.

As Roger Ellsworth has written, 'Christians are not to live in fear of

> If the good news is to be believed then it has to be communicated authentically and clearly, for when God's Word is taught then his voice is heard. God the Holy Spirit takes the Word of God to produce the people of God.

their adversaries, powerful as they may be. Why are we not to give way to fear? Paul gives the following reasons:

THE OPPOSITION OF OUR ADVERSARIES IS TEMPORARY. Their opposition to Christians constitutes opposition to God, and that opposition will finally end in perdition or destruction (2 Thes. 1:6-10).

THE OPPOSITION OF OUR ADVERSARIES PROVES OUR SALVATION. Matthew Henry notes that 'believers have been given two "precious gifts". One is to believe in Christ. The second is to suffer for Christ. The fact that our adversaries cause us to experience the second gift indicates that we have truly received the first. While suffering is never pleasant, it is a privilege and honour to suffer for the Christ who suffered so very much to save his people.'[2]

God's deliverance should be enjoyed (v. 15c)

When you listen to some people, you would think that being a Christian is the pathway to misery and the Christian life is one of restriction instead of liberation. How can the great God, who has created and constantly controls this marvellous universe, be conceived of as a miser? Look around at the rich variety in the created order, the glorious colours he employs and the sheer scope of legitimate enjoyment that he has built into life. He is not a God of drudgery

> How can the great God, who has created and constantly controls this marvellous universe, be conceived of as a miser?

and the mundane, is he? Also, he created us with the capacity for enjoyment. We can laugh and smile and derive great pleasure from so many things. So, resist the temptation to reduce the sheer glory of life.

Rejoicing in your festivals

Nahum tells the people of Judah to rejoice when they hear of Nineveh's overthrow. The news of victory will be proclaimed and it should be openly welcomed throughout the land because they will not be locked up in their towns and cities by a besieging army. Therefore, get out and celebrate the festivals that Moses describes in the law of God.

This, of course, will be a tremendous witness to all who hear what God has done for them. So, they are to keep the worship and praise at a premium, for the Lord will do a wonderful thing for them. They must not go beyond what God prescribes for worship, but within what he has laid down there is great scope for freedom and praise.

> The victory that God gives to his people is eternal.

Treasures on earth

What a contrast to all earthly conquerors, which, at best, only enjoy limited victory. It is true that some empires, like the Ancient Egyptian, Assyrian, Roman or British did have long periods of dominance. But where are they today? They come and they go; but the victory that God gives to his people is eternal.

The people of Judah were told a great thing about the

Assyrians, in general, and about Nineveh, in particular: 'No more will the wicked invade you; they will be completely destroyed.' I wonder how many timid, or fearful, people there were that found this too much to bear, too great a thing to hope for? Yet God was moving and when the end of that great city would be proclaimed across the ancient Near East, the people of Judah were not to be last in appreciating what God had done.

> **And Christian, rejoice! For sin and Satan will not have eternal dominance over you.**

The best is yet to be

Not only do Christians have the joy of knowing that their sins are forgiven in this life, but they will also enter the eternal life of peace and joy that God has promised to all who love him.

Too many people have a jaundiced view about the next life, in which they see a believer clothed in a white garment and sitting on clouds, twanging a harp. It is easy to forget that God created this world that we enjoy so much, despite its sin-marred imperfections. So, will the new one, the home of righteousness, be inferior?

People of Judah, rejoice! The Assyrians will be no more. And Christian, rejoice! For sin and Satan will not have eternal dominance over you. When these things are thought through, it does seem strange, does it not, that we do not rejoice more as believers, for the best is yet to be. Praise God!

FOR FURTHER STUDY

1. Read, or re-read, John Bunyan's book, *The Pilgrim's Progress*, and marvel at the great skill that story teller has in showing how Christ secures the future for his pilgrims.

2. In Isaiah 54:17 and Jeremiah 30:11 we discover the wonderful preservation that God gives to his people. Why were these promises given to these two prophets? Are we able to apply their words to our situations?

TO THINK ABOUT AND DISCUSS

1. The people of Judah were told to rejoice because they would be saved. How should Christians rejoice today without appearing to be triumphalistic or arrogant?

2. Psalm 34 has been used to bring comfort to the distressed. How many of the words of David are applicable today?

3. Many Christians believe that Sunday, The Lord's Day, is a gift from God, that has been given for worshipping him and for the fellowship of his people. By referring to the Bible, how do you think Christians should spend Sundays?

4. The Christian's hope is spoken of in many places in the Bible. Read Isaiah 65:17-25; 1 Corinthians 15:51-58; 2 Corinthians 4:16-5:10 and Revelation 21:1-4 and work through and apply the many wonderful promises given by God.

6 God's acts in the siege of Nineveh

(2:1-6)

There are many laws that govern creation, the law of gravity being an obvious one. But the Bible says that God has also placed another law into man's life and it is stated clearly in Galatians 6:7-8: 'Do not be deceived: God cannot be mocked. A man reaps what he sows. The one who sows to please his sinful nature, from that nature will reap destruction.'

They had a cunning plan

The Assyrians did not become the conquering nation they were by sitting back and letting everything happen around them. They were very skilled at the art of siege warfare and the same way that they assaulted many others would now be the way that God would act against them.

The Assyrian army had a fourfold attack plan that they had honed to a fine art when tackling a fortified stronghold.

It was *isolation, preparation, penetration* and *suppression.* Nahum clearly warns them that they would shortly experience these selfsame things.

The isolation that Nineveh would experience (vv. 1-2)

When laying siege to a city, the ancient Assyrians would seek to isolate the city in order to stop any outside help coming to the inhabitants' aid. So, roads or highways would be blocked, rivers patrolled and escape routes nullified. Nahum describes these things in the opening two verses.

Nineveh is to make sure that she is guarded, that the road is under surveillance and she is to steel herself for the coming enemy.

John Trapp writes, 'The Assyrians have spoiled and pillaged till they have left neither men nor means behind them; such clean works they have made, sweeping all before them, like a sweeping rain that leaves no food (Proverbs 28:3).'[1]

> When laying siege to a city, the ancient Assyrians would seek to isolate the city in order to stop any outside help coming to the inhabitans' aid. So, roads or highways would be blocked, rivers patrolled and escape routes nullified.

We can imagine the sense of panic spreading throughout the city as the defenders looked out and saw the smoke from the enemy's cooking-fires hugging the ground like early morning mist and then the war drums with their terrifying beat sounding like the sound of distant thunder, heralding the coming assault. It would have been enough to make the stoutest heart weak. So, be ready, Nineveh, for you will experience these things.

The preparation that would be made by their enemies (v. 3)

The approach to the defence walls was prepared by levelling the ground to enable the assault troops greater flexibility and manoeuvrability.

Nahum is able to give specific details of the preparations that the enemies would make because God had revealed them to him in advance of the siege taking place.

First impressions are the strongest and the citizens of Nineveh would be terrified by the sight of the approaching army. It was as if Nahum were saying, 'How will you know if this is the last assault against you? Well, look out for these clear signs and details.'

'THE SHIELDS OF HIS SOLDIERS ARE RED'—perhaps covered in this colour to intimidate.

'THE WARRIORS ARE CLAD IN SCARLET'—to show that they are coming to shed blood.

'THE METAL ON THE CHARIOTS FLASHES'—they are blinding in the sun's rays.

'THE SPEARS OF PINE ARE BRANDISHED'—strong, sure and deadly.

When the hoards came against them, there would be no doubt that the end was near. Yet instead of making adequate preparations or fleeing to another place, they stayed where they were and did nothing.

A frightening penetration of Nineveh will happen (v. 4)

In the previous verse, the activity of the enemy forces outside the walls of Nineveh is shown. Now the scene dramatically shifts to inside the walls when the enemy has broken through and the overthrow has begun. The enemy overruns the main thoroughfares and it will be impossible to go anywhere without the inhabitants being in danger. Indeed, many would have been too terrified to move, as the awesome sight of the chariots struck fear into their hearts and minds.

What Nahum describes here is a full-bloodied assault on a city where no quarter is given and no prisoners are taken.

> Many would have been too terrified to move, as the awesome sight of the chariots struck fear into their hearts and minds.

Total suppression will come and the king will be helpless (vv. 5-6)

After these things, the Assyrian army will seek to suppress the defenders by employing the maximum concentration of firepower and superiority of numbers. This will happen at Nineveh. The Assyrian king commits his 'picked troops', perhaps those who have comprised his personal body guard, to the fight. A note of desperation is sounded: 'They dash to the city wall!' Will they get there before it is too late? Even though the protective shield is in place, it is all to no avail, for 'the river gates are thrown open and the palace collapses'.

The ancient historian, Diodorus Siculus, said 'that due to

heavy rainfall and the rise of the rivers Tigris and Khosr, the floodgates were overrun and a section of the city wall dissolved, enabling the Babylonian and Medes to enter the city'[2].

What is interesting to contemplate today is not only the warning that was given, but the detail that was revealed to the Ninevites of God's activity. It is as though the Nazis in 1944 or Saddam Hussein in 2003 had been given detailed plans of how the allies would assault them. Even though the Ninevites had these battle plans, there was nothing they could do to stop the advance of the enemy and the complete fulfilment of God's judgement upon them.

The walls of Nineveh would be broken and her people would perish by the sword, for the throne of empire was cast down and the mighty would be but dust.

> It is as though the Nazis in 1944 or Saddam Hussein in 2003 had been given detailed plans of how the allies would assault them.

Look, listen and learn

So, very clearly in these verses in Nahum we can see how God was going to bring judgement on Nineveh. That is precisely what happened.

In the same way that Nahum did, Jesus too warned the people of his day about the coming destruction of Jerusalem and how violent and awful it would be. But history repeated itself; they did not make adequate preparation or flee to another place and the end came violently in AD 70 (see Luke 21:5-36).

Also, throughout the New Testament, the warning is clearly given that Jesus is coming again to usher in the great Day of Judgement, when, if Jesus is not your Saviour and his precious blood has not covered and atoned for your sin, then you too will discover that your own efforts to save yourself have not been good enough.

Again, what is surprising is how many follow the Ninevites and the Jews by choosing to ignore these warnings!

> The warning is clearly given that Jesus is coming again to usher in the great Day of Judgement, when, if Jesus is not your Saviour and his precious blood has not covered and atoned for your sin, then you too will discover that your own efforts to save yourself have not been good enough.

For further study ▶

FOR FURTHER STUDY

1. Read Galatians 6:1-10 to see how our actions will bring results, either good or evil!

2. Read Philippians 4:8-9 to learn about correct thinking and action.

TO THINK ABOUT AND DISCUSS

1. When God judged the Assyrians, they could understand, if they chose to, why he did it the way he did. Can you see God adopting the same approach today by operating in ways that people can understand? Can you think of any examples?

2. 'As long as we do not hurt others, can we not do as we please?' is the philosophy of many. How would you, as a Christian, seek to challenge and correct that mindset?

3. In Luke 6:37-42 Jesus warned about having a judgemental spirit. How can his words be applied today so that we do not appear as hypocrites who say one thing and do another?

7 God allows the sack of Nineveh

(2:7-10)

Nahum is called upon to give explicit details of how God will deal with the city of Nineveh, so that no cynic can claim that it was just coincidence that the city fell as Nahum had prophesied it would.

The rabbit syndrome

It is very strange that rabbits caught in car headlights at night often freeze and remain motionless on the road. Is it fascination with the intense light, or confusion with something alien to their normal existence confronting them that causes such a reaction? Scholarly opinion is divided on the subject. But the reality is that unless the driver is able to manoeuvre out of the animal's way, another mascot will be added to the front of the car!

Here, in this verse, it is as though the Ninevites will be stunned into inactivity with a sense of 'this cannot be happening to us', when they are caught in the headlights of

God's judgement upon them. So it was that for all their lofty achievements in science and literature, when the end came, the inhabitants of Nineveh also were rooted to the spot and did not escape the judgement that fell. It was a great object lesson to all who witnessed or heard about these momentous happenings to learn that the favour of the powerful was such a fragile thing, for the ground beneath the Ninevites was just paper thin!

God has clearly spoken (v. 7)

> The Bible clearly reveals in numerous places the power of God's Word and its potency, and it is of immense benefit to be reminded of its supremacy.

This verse opens with an emphatic statement and it is one full of meaning: 'It is decreed.' Although scholars debate the precise meaning of the Hebrew word here, decreed is as good as any suggested and the context clearly shows that this decree, this word is from God himself. The Bible clearly reveals in numerous places the power of God's Word and its potency, and it is of immense benefit to be reminded of its supremacy.

GOD'S WORD CREATED ALL THINGS (Gen. 1:3).

GOD'S WORD DESTROYED ALL LIFE AT THE FLOOD, except those in the ark (Gen. 6:7).

GOD'S WORD SUSTAINS ALL LIFE (Matt. 4:4; Heb. 1:3).

GOD'S WORD PRESERVES LIFE FOR THE COMING DAY OF JUDGEMENT (2 Peter 3:7).

GOD'S WORD WILL BRING IN THAT DAY OF JUDGEMENT
(1 Thes. 4:16a).
GOD'S WORD WILL RESURRECT THE DEAD (John 5:28-29).
GOD'S WORD WILL ASSIGN ETERNAL DESTINIES (Matt. 25:41-46).
Just as the people of Nineveh had carried away into exile countless numbers, so they are told that God is going to deal with them in exactly the same way, and they would never return to their home. Indeed, there will not be a home to return to for it will vanish from off the face of the earth.

The picture painted by Nahum is one of anguish and sorrow as the city is laid low, never to rise again.

God's actions are irresistible (v. 8)

This is the first time that Nahum actually mentions Nineveh in his prophecy. In previous verses, the name is put in brackets by Bible translators to help us as we read his book.

What a very dramatic scene is predicted here by Nahum. Can you imagine what it must have been like to see all their hopes disappearing like snow on a summer's morning? Nineveh had as an added protection a branch of the mighty Tigris River along its western walls. But they will see the river bed as the flow dries up.

This actually happened and the physical reality will mirror the mental state of the inhabitants. They audibly cry out in frustration and hopelessness to one another, 'Stop! Stop!' It is as though voicing their pain will bring relief, but none comes. For who would dare to turn back when a split second's indecision may cost a life! They run. But it is too late for the judgement is not turned back.

God will bring ruin to Nineveh (v. 9)

As none turns to defend the walls, the attackers are able to move in swiftly and take up the positions they want. How traumatic this must have been because all the effort the Assyrians had expended when stripping other lands and cities clean to enrich their lives on the goods and possessions of others, was now all for nothing.

Many Assyrian monarchs boasted openly about the vast treasure they had plundered from other nations. How enormous this treasure must have been, not only what they had stripped from others but also what had flowed in each year as they received annual tributes—the price demanded to keep their armies at bay. Over the centuries, they must have accumulated a phenomenal quantity. From this verse, it would appear to be so great that none could count it.

So, again, God causes Nahum to speak of the very things that their rampaging armies had done to others which would now be visited on the Assyrians, in general, and the Ninevites, in particular.

The rape of Nineveh (v. 10)

One of the biggest fears that many women have is that of being attacked at night as they walk home. The horror of being grabbed, thrown to the ground and repeatedly punched, then raped is a nightmare scenario. Although it should not happen, it is, sadly, a frequent occurrence in society today. Here we are given a graphic description of those whose hopes have run out because they had been attacked and were being overwhelmed by a stronger force.

Three words are used to convey the fate that came upon them, and there is a progression as each speaks of the increasing devastation that came with the final assault on Nineveh.

Nineveh was

PILLAGED—the city was despoiled and her beauty taken away;

PLUNDERED—it was ransacked, anything of value was removed or broken up;

STRIPPED—nothing of any use was left; and this was one of their own policies being visited upon them.

The city was sacked and the people reacted in shock and horror at the drama unfolding before their very eyes. It took many long centuries for others to comprehend the severity of the judgement that had fallen upon them; it only came to light with the help of the archaeologist's spade.

> Nothing they could do or say could stop the onset of God's judgement descending upon them. It was too late, just like it was for the lookout on the maiden voyage of the Titanic, who realized too that nothing could be done to avoid colliding with the iceberg.

Remember the Titanic

Nothing they could do or say could stop the onset of God's judgement descending upon them. It was too late, just like it was for the lookout on the maiden voyage of the Titanic, who realized too that nothing could be done to

> The Lord Jesus constantly warned that judgement will come on the earth. But with the passage of time, his words appear to have lost their urgency for many people.

avoid colliding with the iceberg. So it was with Nineveh. The city would sink without trace, and as with the Titanic, only the dedicated endeavours of a few intrepid explorers would give a glimpse of its former majesty.

The Lord Jesus constantly warned that judgement will come on the earth. But with the passage of time, his words appear to have lost their urgency for many people.

FOR FURTHER STUDY

1. Psalm 7:14-16 instructs all who follow the way of evil to remember that their actions will bring a reaction from God. Can you think of other parts of the Bible that carry the same message?

2. In Revelation 16:1-21 God clearly warns all people that he will punish sin. Are these words going to be fulfilled literally or are they just symbolic?

TO THINK ABOUT AND DISCUSS

1. Nahum has been accused of delighting in the sorrows of others. After reading these verses, is there a way that you could defend what he has been saying?

2. How would you seek to share the warnings given in Psalm 7 and Revelation 16 (listed above) with your friends, colleagues at work, family members, etc.—so that they would not dismiss them as idle fancy?

3. Are we sensitive to the sufferings that others endure and what could we do to help those in need? What is a truly Christian response to such suffering?

8 God controls the overthrow of Nineveh

(2:11-13)

Nahum uses a powerful word picture that would have connected with the Ninevites because of their religious beliefs. Almighty God works in ways that people can understand even though they will not always approve of his actions.

Nineveh's rulers were overcome (vv. 11-12)

One of the main deities that the ancient Assyrians worshipped was Ishtar, the goddess of love and war (probably more accurate to say, sex and violence). The planet Venus was connected with her. Her symbol was the eight-pointed star and her sacred ceremonial animal was the lion.

Lions have always attracted attention. Their majesty, colour, manes and power, all lead to kingly comparisons being readily made. Some years ago, I was in a car at Woburn Abbey wildlife park. We had come to a standstill because a young male lion was lying in the road. It lazily looked at us, rose to its feet and stood facing the car. It then lifted one paw and placed it gently on the front of the car causing the car to leap violently. We were grateful for the intervention of a park keeper and none of the passengers was left in any doubt as to the power of that animal. What a suitable emblem for Nineveh, power and might. Who in their right mind would resist?

The ritual lion hunt took place at the New Year festival when the king acted out a number of symbolic roles, including the killing of lions outside the walls of Nineveh. This was a public performance to show that the king was able to protect his subjects from evil. Wall reliefs found in the North Palace of Ashurbanipal at Nineveh show eighteen lions being released in a stacked out area, because Nineveh had eighteen main gates and the king was going to show how in the slaughter of those lions he was powerful enough to protect the city from evil invaders and also to maintain the safety of the approach roads. It does seem peculiar that, if the king alone was indeed fit to preserve peace, no one seems to have questioned why it was necessary to have such a large number of spearmen with him in the enclosure!

Nineveh's destiny was sealed (v. 13a)

The population of Nineveh was probably indifferent to outside threats as it considered itself to be invincible. As in the days of Jonah, so now, whatever threats may be made, in the end a solution would be found and life could continue for them. But they had left one vital factor out of their equation of life.

God the enemy

It is a fearful thing to have God as an enemy and judge. Yet he clearly says to them, 'So far and no further.' It is not just about ignoring United Nations' sanctions. Here is a lawgiver that is also an enforcer. You will learn the lesson, Nineveh, that God cannot and will not be ignored.

> The Bible makes it plain and clear that the greatest need of all people is not justice but mercy, for if God dealt out justice to all, everyone would be condemned.

Speaking about the Day of Judgement to come someone said, 'All I want is justice from God!' The Bible makes it plain and clear that the greatest need of all people is not justice but mercy, for if God dealt out justice to all, everyone would be condemned. We need a Saviour, someone to stand in the way, to take the full force of God's wrath against sin, and that is what Jesus did on the cross.

Nineveh's resources will be destroyed (v. 13b)

The things that the people relied upon would go, for the only safe and sure hope is God himself.

From this description, Nahum's readers are to understand that not only was the Assyrian war machine going to be put out of action, but they would never again be able to terrorize the world. Its chariots were depicted in many wall murals as being large, fearsome and powerful, but they were to go up in smoke. The young lions, their elite soldiers, would not be able to resist and they would be hunted and cut down by the edge of the sword.

Nineveh's voice will be silenced (v. 13c)

The messengers of Assyria were fearsome and frightening, and were cunning in the art of giving seemingly innocuous messages that carried such awful threats. For an example of how they operated read Isaiah 36:13-20, when the commander of Sennacherib's forces spoke in this crafty way outside the walls of Jerusalem. Yet God is not silent and before the Assyrian commander had said anything outside Jerusalem, he had spoken a great word forecasting the shattering of Assyrian might and domination (see Isa. 30:31). So those who were so often the heralds of woe and doom are going to be silenced for ever.

William Makepeace Thackeray said, 'We sow a thought and reap a word, we sow a word and reap a work, we sow a work and reap a habit, we sow a habit and reap a character, we sow a character and reap a destiny!'[1] How true this was for the people of Assyria and they were going to learn the solemn lesson that for all that they had sown, their destiny would be one of destruction and doom.

We are all doomed!

In the BBC's classic comedy series, *Dad's Army*, based on the Home Guard in the Second World War, there is the character Private Frasier. He supposedly originated in the wilds of the North of Scotland and had an austere outlook on life.

Whenever a difficult situation arose, he gave voice to his feelings in using his catch phrase, 'We are doomed, doomed.' Because of this he has been likened to a modern Jeremiah, always bleak in his assessment of any situation.

Correction! Not all are doomed.

Dr John Conder has the following inscription on his tomb in Bunhill Fields, Central London: 'I have sinned—I have trusted—I have repented—I have loved—I rest—I shall rise—and through the grace of Christ, however unworthy—I shall reign.' That is the great hope for all who have confessed their sins and put their trust in the blood of Christ to cleanse them from sin—there is full and free forgiveness.

> Nineveh stands as a great object lesson. For all its pomp and circumstance, it now lies in ruins.

Nevertheless, the choice is clearly laid before mankind: follow God and be free, or follow your own leading and be condemned. Nineveh stands as a great object lesson. For all its pomp and circumstance, it now lies in ruins.

FOR FURTHER STUDY

1. In Revelation 18:9-20 different professions are judged by God. Why do you think that those ones are listed and does this mean that others will be exempt from his wrath?

2. Read the words of Jesus in Luke 13:1-5 where he warns against making rash judgements. Do these verses appear to be discordant with other statements he made?

TO THINK ABOUT AND DISCUSS

1. In Luke 13:1-5 Jesus speaks about atrocities and accidents. How should his words be understood and applied to the events of life today?

2. Many people were justly horrified by the events of 9/11 in New York City in 2001. Why do you think God allowed those aeroplanes to crash into the World Trade Center? Was he judging Western society as he had judged Nineveh?

3. It is a strange thing that many people do not have a thought for God until a disaster occurs. Then, it is not uncommon to hear someone say, 'If God is a God of love, why did he permit that to happen?' What should the Christian's response be to a statement like that?

9 God judges Nineveh's sin

(3:1-7)

The kings of Assyria knew the advantage psychological warfare could give them over their enemies. Many records have survived that tell so clearly and explicitly their use of this frightening form of intimidation to subdue their opponents.

The sin of Nineveh is stated (v. 1)

The last great king of Assyria, Ashurbanipal, wrote about the campaign against Taharqa of Egypt: 'The people who had revolted, I captured. Great and small, I cut down with the sword. Their corpses I hung on stakes. I tore off their skins and covered the wall of the city with them.'[1] Naturally, anyone reading this description would think twice about rebellion against such a nation. These things can be clearly seen on many Assyrian wall panels.

Describing this terrifying practice, Walter Maier wrote,

'The atrocious practice of cutting off hands and feet, ears and noses, gouging out eyes, looping of heads, and then binding them to the vines or heaping them up before city gates; the utter fiendishness by which captives could be impaled or flayed alive through a process in which their skin was gradually and completely removed—this planned frightfulness systematically enforced by the "bloody city" was now to be avenged.'[2]

Why do we never learn?

God's people were not to gloat or to consider themselves superior to Nineveh in any way, as, surprisingly, this description, 'city of blood', is also given twice to Jerusalem by the prophet Ezekiel (24:6,9) after this time and Nahum would have been a reminder to them of what happens to those who stubbornly refuse to repent.

Tragically the lesson was not learnt, for in the New Testament when Jesus surveyed history, he said about Jerusalem's future decimation, 'O Jerusalem, Jerusalem, you who kill the prophets and stone those sent to you, how often I have longed to gather your children together, as a hen gathers her chicks under her wings, but you were not willing! Look, your house is left to you desolate. I tell you, you will not see me again until you say, "Blessed is he who comes in the name of the Lord" '(Luke 13:34-35).

The Jewish people only had to read Nahum and see what happened to Nineveh to discover what would come upon them if they did not show true remorse for their sins.

Assault on Nineveh is described (vv. 2-3)

It must have been a terrifying experience to be in a city under siege. But how much more to have seen the enemy break through and charge after you, intent on delivering pain and almost certain death.

How ghastly this is in all its vivid description of the death throes of Nineveh. As Raymond Brown notes about the whole of Nahum: 'The word of the prophet here seems harsh and pitiless, but one must remember the agony caused throughout the near-eastern world by the Assyrian invaders. They have been described as "the most brutal empire which has ever suffered to roll its forces across the world." The book is about the utter justice of God, and as such, it has an essential place in the Bible. Men must be reminded not only of the goodness, but also of the severity of God (Rom. 2:1-4; 11:22).' 3

Therefore, all can understand God's reason for bringing an end to Nineveh; it is for justice not only to be done, but also to be seen to be done.

Almighty God never has to explain himself. But graciously, so that none can accuse him of being simply vindictive, he states why it is that Nineveh will be humbled.

> Almighty God never has to explain himself. But graciously, so that none can accuse him of being simply vindictive, he states why it is that Nineveh will be humbled.

Why judgement came to Nineveh (v. 4)

The language employed here leaves no doubt as to why it was that God acted in the way he did for in the Bible, witchcraft, necromancy, and the black arts are roundly condemned. The Spirit world is unfamiliar territory for earth-bound human beings and dealing with unknown forces is extremely dangerous. God alone knows what is good and right, and he warns any who meddle in these things that they are taking a terrible risk and are going against him. Nineveh's people followed their leaders, and King Esarhaddon, especially, was noted as a superstitious and almost neurotic man who surrounded himself with soothsayers, priests and magicians.

> God alone knows what is good and right, and he warns any who meddle in these things that they are taking a terrible risk ...

So God judges Nineveh severely, and what happened to those people is a warning to all who go against him and his Word.

God is actively against the city (vv. 5-7)

It is desperately sad when someone is left all alone in the world, with no companion or friend either to share things with or just to have around if needed. Yet that is the picture that is now presented of the fate of this great city and its inhabitants. Total embarrassment was going to be their lot for they delighted in humiliating and dehumanizing others. Now, as judgment falls, they learn what it is like to be those who are devoid of compassion. The Assyrian king, Ashurbanipal, tells how he had captured Uaite: 'I pierced his chin with my keen hand dagger. Through his jaw I passed a rope, put a dog chain upon him and made him occupy a kennel of the east gate of the wall of Nineveh, which is named Entrance of the Thronging Nations. To the glory of Assur, Isthar and the great gods, my lords, I took pity upon him, and spared his life.' 4 Not many would agree that that is real pity, only degradation and complete humiliation.

> **Kingdoms may rise and kingdoms do fall, but God goes on for ever.**

Another history lesson

Austen Henry Layard said of the discoveries he made, 'For twenty-five centuries these sculptures had been hidden from the eye of man, and they now stand forth once more in their ancient majesty. But how changed is the scene around them! The luxury and civilization of a mighty nation has given place to the wretchedness and ignorance of a few half-barbarous tribes. The wealth of temples, and the riches of great cities, have been succeeded by ruins and shapeless heaps of earth. Above the spacious hall, in which they stood, the plough has passed and the corn now waves.'

They had been covered by earth, dirt and debris, lost and forgotten; but the God of the Bible cannot be buried out of sight for he always lives and is intimately active in the affairs of this world. Kingdoms may rise and kingdoms do fall, but God goes on for ever.

FOR FURTHER STUDY

1. In Isaiah 36:1-20 another example of Assyrian psychological warfare is given. Why is it that the mind is often attacked before physical violence takes place?

2. Israel's first king, Saul, consulted a medium. Read about it and the effect it had on him in 1 Samuel 28:1-25. Where else does the Bible warn about the forces of the occult and the Christian's need to avoid such things?

TO THINK ABOUT AND DISCUSS

1. The Assyrians were bullies. Sadly, today, we often hear about the effect bullying has in the school and the workplace. What should the Christian's response be to such behaviour. How can we help victims of abuse?

2. Why is there such diversity in standards of living across the world and does this show that God does not care about the majority of the earth's population?
In the aftermath of the fall of Saddam Hussein and the Barth party in Iraq in 2004, many disturbing images of allied troops abusing Iraqis have been published. Is there any justification whatsoever for abusing prisoners?

3. Many shocking cases of genocide have taken place in the last fifty years. What should the Christian's response be to the wholesale slaughter of people groups?

10 God compares Nineveh to Thebes

(3:8-11)

Recent history is used by God when he compares Nineveh to the Egyptian city of Thebes to teach the Assyrians a great lesson. Would they learn or did they care, for who could stop them?

God asks the people of Nineveh a question (vv. 8-9)

In the Bible we learn that God is someone who communicates with people. He is described as the speaking God, (see page 62) and he takes the initiative here to ask the inhabitants of Nineveh a question. It is couched in a way that requires an answer.

Many people like to think of themselves as superior to others and God uses this to elicit a response, 'Are you better than Thebes?' he asks them, as he brings to their minds an event from their recent history.

The city of Thebes spoken of here was the one in Egypt and not the one in Greece. It was a fabulous place and the ancient remains that can be visited today speak of a long and rich past. It is still possible to walk its sun-scorched streets and along the sphinx-lined processional ways to the temples. When the nation was united and strong in the New Kingdom era, the Pharaoh would receive the crown in the temple of Karnak, the largest known place of worship in the ancient world. It was to this place that death, defeat and humiliation came when the armies of Assyria laid siege to it with great ferocity.

New king, old ways

At the head of that army was Ashurbanipal, the last great king of Assyria who succeeded to the throne when his father, Esarhaddon, died on his way to a campaign in Egypt in 669 BC. His death caused the Pharaoh, Taharqa, whom Sennacherib's spokesman had called thirty-two years earlier 'that splintered reed of a staff, which pierces a man's hand and wounds him if he leans on it!' (Isaiah 36:6), to launch an offensive against the Assyrian garrison stationed at Memphis in 667 BC. Ashurbanipal sent his rapid response units against him and reclaimed the lost territory by the use of force. As their long history often reveals, the ancient Egyptians were patient and persistent. Four years later in 663 BC, when Taharqa's nephew, Tantamnni, had become Pharaoh, the Egyptians tried again to regain control of Memphis and the Delta region, which was being governed by Assyrian vassal rulers.

In response to this, Ashurbanipal reacted with another invasion. This time he did not stop in the north of Egypt but pushed down the Nile to the great capital of Upper Egypt, Thebes.

The dreadful scenes in Thebes (v. 10)

As ever, it is the weak and innocent who suffer most when trouble comes.

Despite its long history and stout defences, the Egyptians and their ancient city were no match for the might of the Assyrian army. The city capitulated and its treasures were looted and many of its people were deported to Assyria. Margaret Murray tells how Ashurbanipal struck fear into the Egyptian population and quotes him, 'My army took the whole of Thebes; silver, gold, precious stones, the furniture of the palace, costly and beautiful garments, great horses, men and women; two lofty obelisks covered with beautiful carving, which were set up before the gate of a temple, I wrenched and brought to Assyria.' She then adds the comment, 'This was the terrible sack of Thebes which sent a shudder of horror through all the countries within Assyria.' [1]

Not known for leniency the Assyrians had taught the citizens of Thebes a brutal lesson and it caused many a tear to be shed in anguish and pain. The graphic details here make sickening reading. As ever, it is the weak and innocent who suffer most when trouble comes.

The Egyptians, Necho and his son Psamtik, were left in charge of Egypt by Ashurbanipal. But eventually, they too asserted their independence in 656 BC. Only this time Ashurbanipal did not return.

Measure for measure (v. 11)

Just as others had not known what to do when the Assyrians turned up on their doorsteps, so now the table will be turned and the Assyrians will lose control. Drunk, disorientated, confused and frightened, they will run for their lives pursued by the enemy.

A crime writer learns a lesson

Sir Max Mallowan, the second husband of Agatha Christie (the famous crime writer), was a famous Assyriologist. He once said to his wife, 'Archaeology is really quite like whodunits——we use similar methods.'

He proved his point to her when demonstrating the disintegration of the Assyrian Empire two years before the fall of Nineveh at the site of ancient Nimrud. Agatha watched in fascination as he pieced together a tale of murder and plunder in that ancient city. He had traced the unmistakable signs of a drunken mob, rampaging through the streets. 'But how did you know they were drunk?' she asked.

'Elementary, my dear Agatha,' Sir Max replied, 'they did not burn the wine cellars.'[2]

So, these facts of Assyrian history came about and uncontrollable drunken mobs could run riot through the once proud cities of that mighty empire.

History comes alive

The former dictator of Iraq, Saddam Hussein, was eventually tracked down and discovered to be hiding in a hole in the ground. He was supposedly defiant to the last and, as he was dragged out, uttered the words, 'I am Saddam Hussein, President of Iraq, and I wish to negotiate.'3 If it were not so serious, it would have appeared comical to see this man, feared and hated by so many, now dishevelled and dirty, thinking that he had any bargaining power with the troops of the dominant superpower in the world.

> Satan, like every other being who sets himself up as a rival to the one and only God, will have a day of reckoning to face, and he will be exposed for the liar and usurper he truly is.

About fifty years before Nahum's prophecy, Isaiah said that about the king of Babylon: 'Those who see you stare at you, they ponder your fate: "Is this the man who shook the earth and made kingdoms tremble, the man who made the world a desert, who overthrew its cities and would not let his captives go home?"' (Isaiah 14:16,17).

Using the three levels of understanding described on page 12, many think that Isaiah was describing not only a human king but also the false king Satan, the Devil himself. On the great day of the Lord, like Saddam Hussein and the king of Babylon, people will stare in bewilderment and exclaim, 'Is that what he is truly like, the one who terrified many?'

Satan, like every other being who sets himself up as a rival to the one and only God, will have a day of reckoning to face, and he will be exposed for the liar and usurper he truly is. Nineveh and her kings also offer us an object lesson of these things. The way they have gone, the devil will go, banished for ever to his eternal fate.

For further study ▶

FOR FURTHER STUDY

1. Read 2 Kings 6:24 - 7:20 and Joel 2:6-9 to see how dreadful siege warfare was in the ancient world. Where else does the Bible speak about war and peace and the Christian's response to these things?

2. Jesus said in John 12:8 that there would always be poor people on earth. Are we able to establish a biblical basis for helping the poor and weak?

TO THINK ABOUT AND DISCUSS

1. Nahum is concerned with historical events in Northern Iraq. Can you think of other events in the Bible that have taken place in Iraq?

2. Like Saddam Hussein with the American soldiers, many think that they have qualities with which to bargain with God. What things are there in your life that God might be pleased with?

3. Do you believe in the Devil? If not, why do you think you feel he is not relevant to life in the twenty-first century?

11 God announces Nineveh's doom

(3:12-19)

John Donne (1571–1631) wrote: 'Any man's death diminishes me, because I am involved in Mankind; and therefore never send to know for whom the bell tolls; it tolls for thee.' The solemn sound of the death knell was ringing out for the people of Nineveh, but they were so caught up with their own lives that they had become deaf to its solemn sound.

Nineveh is given a nature lesson (v. 12)

Nineveh had become so vulnerable that with relatively little cost or sacrifice the enemy would take the city. Nothing would stop his progress and to him it would appear as easy as taking a ripe fruit from a tree. The accounts that have survived show the truth of these words and their complete fulfilment.

Nabopolasar, the father of the great Babylonian king, Nebuchadnezzar, was instrumental in the final sack of

Nineveh, and the description of his campaign is on the Babylonian Chronicle which is now in the British Museum in London. It says, 'In the tenth year, Nabopolasar, in the month of Aiaru [March], mobilized the Babylonian army and marched up the banks of the Euphrates. The people of the lands of Suhu and Hinanu did not attack him but laid their tribute before him.' Nabopolasar also wrote, 'I slaughtered the land of Assyria, I turned the hostile land into heaps and ruins. The Assyrian who since distant days had ruled over all the peoples and with a heavy yoke had brought injury to the people of the lands, his yoke I threw off!' In particular, 'At Nineveh a mighty assault against the city and a great slaughter was made of the people and nobles.'

Nineveh's army is insulted (v. 13)

There is no political correctness here, but honest reality: 'Look at your troops—they are all women', effeminate, weaker then the attackers and, in a popular phrase of a previous generation, 'You are a bunch of Nancy boys!' This helps to explain the strange phenomenon of Nineveh's rapid defeat. Egypt besieged Ashdod for twenty-nine years, and Ashdod was very small in comparison to Nineveh, yet in three months it had fallen.

Trial by fire (vv. 14-15)

The reality of this can be seen in Room 9 of the British Museum. There the wall stone reliefs from Sennacherib's Palace without Rival show the scorching effects of the fire that engulfed the city at the end and they are badly cracked and scarred by the heat as a consequence.

Relatively recent excavations have shown that the city's defenders narrowed the width of the northern Adad Gate and the south-western Halzi Gate from seven to two metres, in a desperate attempt to render them more defensible. The discovery of the skeletons of many guards close to the gates—with evidence of parry blows to the arms, thrust wounds to the chest, and arrows embedded in the bones—is testimony to the savagery of the final assault when it came.[1]

Locust power (vv. 16-17)

Locusts are rightly feared in many places for their rapacious appetite. The after-effect of an invasion is one of total devastation and heartbreak; nothing is left and many years of hard work can disappear in an instant.

> The after-effect of an invasion is one of total devastation and heartbreak; nothing is left and many years of hard work can disappear in an instant.

With the considerable bargaining power of their army behind, the greedy merchants spread far and wide, stripping resources from many and sowing salt in the fields so that, like a locust swarm, devastation followed in their wake. But they became slack. They thought all places were easy pickings and this undermined their strength and awareness of the world situation.

False shepherds (v. 18)

> When God finally settles accounts, he settles them in full. All people on earth would do well to learn this solemn but real truth, for now is the day of salvation, tomorrow may be too late.

A title of many Assyrian monarchs was 'Great Shepherd of the people'. They boasted of their power to protect their people but, in reality, like many, the leaders and those under them sought to preserve their own skins before seeing to the people in their care.

It is one of the ironies of history that one part of the ruins of Nineveh is called Tell Kuyunjik, which means 'The mound of many sheep'. How the mighty have fallen! In the place of kings are shepherds; and in the place of people are sheep!

Look at the Great Shepherd

What a tremendous contrast the New Testament gives us when we come face to face with the great Shepherd of the sheep, the Lord Jesus Christ. He did not just speak of his task but showed by what he did that he truly cares for his people.

Rejoicing as she dies (v. 19)

The city was dying from an incurable wound and it was an occasion for joy and not sadness. No doubt, there were many who would have gloated over the shocking events of her passing. God's people should be different and realize that it was a fulfilment of his Word and, therefore, the song of praise should be raised to him for protecting his people.

In Nineveh's destruction there was none to be found who mourned her passing. 'The fate of Nineveh had hung over the city for centuries, and was long delayed, but over its ruins might well be written the words: "The mills of God grind slowly, but they grind, exceedingly small." When God finally settles accounts, he settles them in full.'[2]

Is Nahum describing ethnic cleansing?

No one sat on the ruins of Nineveh to write a lament over its passing. In time its very existence was queried, such was the obliteration it suffered as a consequence of the word and action of God.

Many other smaller cities took far longer to capitulate. For instance, Samaria, the capital of Israel, was taken by the Assyrians after a three year siege (2 Kings 18:10).

When God finally settles accounts, he settles them in full. All people on earth would do well to learn this solemn but real truth, for now is the day of salvation, tomorrow may be too late.

> When God finally settles accounts, he settles them in full.

It is amazing that two of the Minor Prophets should be devoted to Nineveh; its importance in the ancient world is reflected in the prominence the biblical writers give to it and its destiny.

Jonah's prophecy on Nineveh concludes in a very different fashion from that of Nahum's, for in Jonah God says, 'Should I not be concerned about that great city?' (Jonah 4:11). The city is the same but this time there is going to be a very different result, for God's patience has run out, and Nineveh must be destroyed. God's incomprehensible mercy had been revealed through Jonah and his unimaginable wrath through Nahum.

> God's incomprehensible mercy had been revealed through Jonah and his unimaginable wrath through Nahum.

God's undeserved mercy had been seen in saving his people and his awesome vengeance in punishing his enemies. In this we are given a foreshadowing of what it will be like on the great day of Christ's Second Coming. When he appears, may we, by his grace and mercy, find ourselves warmed by his love and not the recipients of the fire of his wrath.

J. Sidlow Baxter gives the following warning to his readers: 'Let the peoples of today take a long, steady, thoughtful look at old-time Nineveh. She is one of God's special object-lessons to all rulers and nations. It is the same God who super-rules the world today. He is not less severe than he was in the Old Testament times, and he is not more compassionate. He is just as uncompromising towards sin, just as compassionate towards the penitent, the same from age to age. The idea that the Gospel of Christ somehow tones down the severity in the divine character is wrong. Certainly, the gospel is the supreme expression of the Divine graciousness; but it does not in the slightest degree modify the inflexible principles of righteousness by which God governs nations. God has always been gracious. God has always been intolerant of wickedness. He is the same today.' 3

God has always been intolerant of wickedness. He is the same today.

For further study ▶

FOR FURTHER STUDY

1. Read what Jesus says in Matthew 25:41 about the fire that will be experienced by many who do not love him.

2. Then, by way of comparison, read Jesus' words in John 14:1-4 about the warmth of God's love.

TO THINK ABOUT AND DISCUSS

1. Life is very brief and, although, when we are young time can drag, as we grow older it appears to speed up. How can we alert others to the need to use time wisely and to prepare for the future?

2. Is the supposed gloating of Nineveh's fate something that appals you? Why do you suppose that God gave such a tough message to Nahum?

3. Many people consider the Second Coming of Jesus to be either wishful thinking or an irrelevance. How do you view this subject? Do you think Nahum helps us to focus on the parts of God's Word that have yet to be fulfilled?

12 History's verdict on Nahum and Nineveh

If God's Word is to be believed, then it has to be seen to be real and relevant, and to have power to affect the course of life itself. So what should we make of the compelling evidence that shows this prophecy has been fulfilled?

Nineveh is a ruin

The explorer and rediscoverer of Nineveh, Austen Henry Layard, considered it one of the most remarkable facts of his day that the records of an empire, so renowned for its power and civilization, were entirely lost. Nineveh had limited occupation in Hellenistic, Parthian and Roman times, but there was very little left for the inhabitants.

Where has it gone?

So complete was the destruction of Nineveh that in 400 BC, just 212 years after its fall, Xenophon (428 BC -354 BC), the Greek historian who journeyed with 10,000 mercenary soldiers, was unable to discover what site he was on and thought that the ruins were a Median city destroyed by the

Achaemenids. In the twelfth century Benjamin of Tudela had identified opposite Mosul the ruin mounds Tell Kuyunjik and Nebu Yunus (mound of Jonah), where the prophet Jonah is said to be buried. He saw that the city had disappeared and the site was covered with many small villages. In 1575 the German, Leonhart Rauwolff, referred to a 'high round hill' and wrote, 'It is entirely honeycombed, being inhabited by poor people, whom I often saw crawling in and out in large numbers, like ants in their heap. At that place and in the region hereabouts years ago the mighty city of Nineveh was situated.'

> Mistakes had been made by the ancient Assyrians and, like the latter Roman Empire, complacency settled in to the detriment and downfall of all that had been built up.

Sir Anthony Shirley, in the time of Queen Elizabeth I of England, spoke quaintly of, 'Nineveh, that which God himself calls that great City, has not one stone standing which may give memory of the being of a town. One English mile from it is a place called Mosul, a small thing, rather to be a witness of the others mightiness and God's judgement, than of any fashion of magnificence in itself.' Then, at the end of the seventeenth century, Pietro della Valle gave a precise description of the line of the city wall and said, 'It had four sides, not of the same length, nor is it square.'[1]

No room for error

Why had such devastation happened to such a great city? Mistakes had been made by the ancient Assyrians and, like the latter Roman Empire, complacency settled in to the detriment and downfall of all that had been built up.

There are many theories as to why the mighty empire crumbled so quickly and easily, so that one of the great civilizations with a powerful army to protect it could fall so dramatically.

God had also spoken through the prophet Isaiah, saying, 'The voice of the LORD will shatter Assyria; with his sceptre he will strike them down' (Isaiah 30:31). This total destruction caused many to doubt if Nineveh ever existed.

Mr Nasty?

Many writers think Nahum gives an inaccurate view of the Assyrians, so that, in the Bible, they are viewed 'through the distorting lens of a highly ethnocentric and theological view of history presented to us in the pages of the Old Testament.' Or another writes about Nahum saying how 'a yapping Israelite prophet snarled'.[2]

It is sad that many professional archaeologists do not accord to the Bible the same respect they give to other ancient writings. Yet it is contemporaneous with all the other documents that are used to build a picture of life in the ancient world. But, for many, the Bible occupies an inferior position.

The silent stones speak

There was no doubt that it had ceased to be a city and was destined to become an archaeologist's dream, with who knows how many rich finds still to be uncovered. One problem lies in there being so large a mosque covering the mound of Nebi Yunus, for on that site the palace of Esarhaddon is still to be excavated along with many other treasures.

> The fall of Nineveh was really dramatic and serves as a grim warning to the entire world that God keeps his word.

In his book, *The Final sack of Nineveh*, John Malcolm Russell says, 'Sadly, one of the recurring themes in this study is that Sennacherib's palace is no longer what it once was. It is a great shame that the building was destroyed in antiquity, but this was an inevitable consequence of the sack of Nineveh. It is an even greater shame that so much of what remained of the building has been destroyed since its excavation in the nineteenth century.'3

None can doubt that Nahum's words have been fulfilled for the evidence is there for all to see. The fall of Nineveh was really dramatic and serves as a grim warning to the entire world that God keeps his word.

The call for modesty

The Assyriologist, Georges Roux, wisely wrote, 'A glorious past was forgotten. In man's short memory of these opulent cites and mighty monarchs only a few, often distorted, names survived. The dissolving rain, the sand-bearing winds, the earth-splitting sun conspired to obliterate all material remains and the desolate mounds which conceal the ruins of Nineveh offer perhaps the best lesson in modesty that we shall ever receive from history.'4

It is no laughing matter

Many consider that Tony Hancock was among the greats of British comedy. He was often on the television and some of his sketches, like 'The blood donor', have become legendary. He appeared to have everything going for him, but he died of an overdose in Australia in 1968. His last television monologue in 1964 proved to be a sad farewell.

'What have you achieved? What have you achieved? You lost your chance, me old son. You contributed absolutely nothing to this life. A waste of time you being here at all. No place for you in Westminster Abbey. The best you can expect is a few daffodils in a jam jar, a rough-hewn stone bearing the legend "He came and he went" and in between nothing! Nobody will even notice you're not here. After about a year afterwards somebody might say down the pub, "Where's old Hancock? I haven't seen him around lately."

' "Oh, he's dead y'know."

' "Oh, is he?"

'A right raison d'être that is. Nobody will ever know I ever existed. Nothing to leave behind me. Nothing to pass on. Nobody to mourn me. That's the bitterest blow of all.'

How well Hancock sums up the plight of the Ninevites

> The kingdom of God has no end for he secures his people's future, and Nahum challenges us all to consider our standing before him who is the Judge and King of all.

and of all people who have no hope or future.

What is our situation?

As we conclude our look at Nahum, it would be prudent to ask this question: Nineveh and the Assyrian Empire have long gone, but where are God's people today? The apostle Paul, writing in Galatians 3:29, says, 'If you belong to Christ, then you are Abraham's seed, and heirs according to the promise.' The kingdom of God has no end for he secures his people's future, and Nahum challenges us all to consider our standing before him who is the Judge and King of all. For, if we do not experience the warmth of God's love, then we will be the recipients of the fire of his wrath.

FOR FURTHER STUDY

1. Read Zephaniah 2:13-15 and see how that prophet clearly foretold the utter desolation that would come on Nineveh.

2. We are not told how Nahum felt about giving this prophetic word, but if you read Jeremiah 20:7-18, you will discover how that prophet felt about speaking for God. Do we have any hope in our lives, or are we like Tony Hancock, full of despair and dejection?

TO THINK ABOUT AND DISCUSS

1. Nineveh is no more and, therefore, relegated to history. Is it important to read through and study Nahum's prophecy in the present or are we wasting our time going over an old story?

2. As you consider the future, are you filled with hope or despair when you consider that God was actively involved in the destruction of Nineveh?

3. Are there any positive lessons you can draw for your life when considering the vengeance and salvation of God?

4. As you conclude this study, read and discuss the implications of Paul's teaching in Romans 8:18-39 with respect to the future of the Christian believer.

Endnotes

Background and summary
1 Donald J. Wiseman, *Life Above and Below Memoirs*, Privately Published pp. 108-9.
2 Michael Rolf, *Cultural Atlas of Mesopotamia and the Ancient Near East, Facts on File*, pp. 186-91, (For extended details on the history of Nineveh).

Chapter 1
1 C.S. Lewis, *The Lion, The Witch and The Wardrobe*, Penguin p.75

Chapter 3
1 Charles Haddon Spurgeon, *Metropolitan Tabernacle Pulpit, 1898*, Vol. 44, p. 61
2 No. 57 From Olney Hymns, Book 1, based on Song of Solomon 1:3

Chapter 4
1 Brian Edwards, *Revival: A people saturated with God*, Evangelical Press, p. 29
2 Thomas Brooks, *Works, Vol. 3*. The Banner of Truth Trust, pp. 413-4

Chapter 5
1 John Bunyan, *The Pilgrim's Progress in today's English*, retold by James H. Thomas, Victory Press, pp. 113-18.
2 Roger Ellsworth, *Opening up Philippians,* Day One Publications, p. 34.

Chapter 6
1 John Trapp, *Commentary on the Old and New Testaments*, Vol. 4, Tanski publications, p. 314
2 Homer Hailey, *A Commentary on the Minor prophet*s, Religious Supply Inc., p. 261

Chapter 8
1 W. M. Thackeray, *The Penguin dictionary of Quotations*, Bloomsbury Books

Chapter 9
1 Daniel David Luckenball, *Ancient Records of Assyria and Babylonia-Part Two*, Histories and Mysteries of Man
2 Walter Maier, *Nahum*, Concordia, p. 292
3 Raymond Brown, *The Bible book by book,* Marshall Pickering, p.154
4 Austen Henry Layard, *Nineveh and its Remains*, Routledge and Kegan Paul

Chapter 10
1 Margaret A. Murray, *The Splendour that was Egypt*, Book Club Associates, 1973, p.51
2 Arnold C. Brackman, *The Luck of Nineveh,* Eyre Methuen, p. 331
3 BBC News World Edition Website for Monday 15th December 2003

Chapter 11
1 Gwendolyn Leick, *Mesopotamia The Invention of the City*, Penguin Books Ltd, p. 241
2 John Phillips, *Exploring the Scriptures*, Victory Press, p. 143
3 J. Sidlow Baxter, *Explore the book,* Vol. 4, Marshall, Morgan & Scott Ltd, p. 199.

Chapter 12
1 Charlotte Trumper, *Agatha Christie and Archaeology*, The British Museum Press, p. 75
2 H.W.F. Saggs, *The Might that was Assyria,* Sidgwick and Jackson, p. 246
3 John Malcolm Russell, *The Final sack of Assyria,* Yale University Press, p. 49.
4 G. Roux, *Ancient Iraq,* Penguin

Additional resources

Nahum, Tremper Longman III in The Minor Prophets Vol. 2 edited by Thomas Edward McComiskey, Baker Book House, ISBN 0-8010-6307-8

Through the British Museum – with the Bible, Brian Edwards and Clive Anderson, Day One Publications, ISBN 1 903087 54-6

Discoveries from Bible Times, Alan Millard, Lion Publishing, ISBN 0 7324 1608 6

The Bible in the British Museum, T.C. Mitchell, The British Museum Press, ISBN 0-7141-1698-X

Dictionary of the Ancient Near East, Edited by Piotr Bienkowski and Alan Millard, The British Museum Press, ISBN 0-7141-1141-4

On the Reliability of the Old Testament. K. A. Kitchen, Wm. B. Eerdmans Publishing Co., ISBN 0-8028-4960-1

Archaeology and the Old Testament, Alfred J. Hoerth, Baker Book House, ISBN 0-8010-1129-9

Grace–amazing grace. Brian H Edwards, Day One Publications, ISBN 1 903087 55-4

OPENING UP NAHUM

The Opening up series

| Opening up | Opening up | Opening up | Opening up | Opening up |
| Philippians | Ezekiel's visions | 1 Timothy | Nahum | Ecclesiastes |

Further titles in preparartion

This fine series is aimed at the 'average person in the church' and combines brevity, accuracy and readability with an attractive page layout. Thought-provoking questions make the books ideal for both personal or small group use.

> **'Laden with insightful quotes and penetrating practical application, Opening up Philippians is a Bible study tool which belongs on every Christian's bookshelf!'**
> DR. PHIL ROBERTS, PRESIDENT, MIDWESTERN BAPTIST THEOLOGICAL SEMINARY, KANSAS CITY, M I S S O U R I '

Please contact us for a free catalogue

In the UK ☎ 01568 613 740 **email—** sales@dayone.co.uk

In the United States: ☎ Toll Free:1-8–morebooks

In Canada: ☎ 519 763 0339 www.dayone.co.uk